Pugh's Commonplace

A Twentieth-Century
Commonplace Book

OLEANDER

Oleander Press
16 Orchard Street
Cambridge
CB1 1JT

www.oleanderpress.com

A CIP catalogue record for the book is available from the British Library.

ISBN: 9780900891380

Printed in England

Foreword

From 1949 to 1979 Leslie Pugh was first a Congregational Church minister and then a United Reformed Church minister in the North West of England. He preached regularly twice on Sundays for twenty minutes on each occasion and gave numerous evening talks to different groups of church members in his own and other churches. He was an avid reader, both for pleasure and to support his teaching and preaching duties. When, through age and infirmity, he had to be cared for, his house was cleared. Almost the last thing left to go was a little black book filled with tiny handwriting. The family knew nothing of its existence up to this point. On close examination it turned out to be a collection of different quotations from a wide variety of sources that Lesley had gleaned as a resource book for the preparation of the sermons and talks which took up so much of his time. Covering the thirty years that it did, it seemed to me to be of intrinsic interest and value.

This is a copy of that collection of quotations. There are examples taken from classic philosophy and theology, from hymns, from children's poetry, from poems and novels: there are wise men's observations of the simple life of simple folk. Together, they have potential interest to every understanding and outlook and describe, almost unwittingly, the power of non-conformist thought on the lives and ideas of many people during the immediate post war period.

The reader will not find all quotations equally illuminating: how could they? But together they provide insight into the condition of human life in that society and at that time, which may have relevance for them to the human condition in this time. I commend them to the reader.

David Pugh

Rev. Leslie Pugh. 1912 - 2006
Brief Biography

The Reverend Leslie Pugh was born in Keighley, Yorkshire in 1912. He trained as a draughtsman and married Caroline Elizabeth Martin in 1935. They had three children, Margaret, born 1940, David, born 1944 and Susan, born 1947. Before the war Leslie was a member of the Peace Pledge Union and for a short time the Independent Labour Party. During the war he was a conscientious objector and worked mainly on the land. He also packed medical supplies and was a fire watcher in Manchester. After the war he trained as a Congregational Minister and took up his first appointment in 1949 at Breightmet Free Church, Bolton. In 1954 he moved to Droylsden, between Manchester and Ashton-under-Lyne. In 1969 he moved again, this time to Farnworth - Albert Road Congregational Church - though by now, after its union with the Presbyterian Church, it had become United Reformed. His final ministry was at Little Hulton, near Farnworth. He retired from there at the age of 67 in 1979. Carrie died in the same year. After being looked after for many years by Margaret, his final years were spent being cared for in Bolton until his death on December 29th 2006 at the age of 94. He was frail and had lost his mental powers.

These quotations can also be found on the 'allquotes' page of the allonsong. com website (allonsong.com/family).

ACCEPTING/ACCEPTANCE

It was not until he was middle-aged that he (Robert Lynd) could accept presents without actual discourtesy.

Radio Show

We experience moments in which we accept ourselves, because we feel that we have been accepted by that which is greater than we have. If only more such moments were given to us! For it is such moments that make us love our life, that make us accept ourselves, not in our goodness and self-complacency, but in our certainty of the inner meaning of life.

Paul Tillich: *Shaking the Foundations*

Friday: In Dag Hammarskjold's *Markings* there are two entries apropos of the above. In the spring of the year he died he wrote, "I don't know who – or what - put the question. I don't know when it was put. I don't even remembering answering. But at some moment I did answer Yes to Someone - or Something – and from that hour I was certain that existence is meaningful and that, therefore, my life, in self-surrender, had a goal." The other is this: "God does not die on the day we cease to believe in a personal deity, but we die on the day when our lives cease to be illuminated by the steady radiance of a wonder, the source of which is beyond all reason."

Dag Hammarskjold: *Markings* quoted in
Bolton Weekly 17th June 1965

ADVENTURE

The things that haven't been done before
Are the things worthwhile today.
Are you one of the flock that follows or
Are you one that shall lead the way?
Are you one of the timid souls that quail
At the jeers of the doubting crew,
Or dare you, whether you win or fail,
Strike out for the path that's new?

Anon

ANXIETY

Anxiety, the spice of life...
Professor Arnold Toynbee in a lecture at Bryn Mawr College,
Philadelphia, said that the world had "no moral claim" to enjoy political
and economic stability. "Anxiety, insecurity and danger are normal
conditions of human life," he said. "Do not dread or resent the insecurity
that has overtaken the middle classes in the United States and other
English speaking nations. On the contrary, welcome it as an adventure."

Professor Arnold Toynbee
Associated Press cutting.

He (Dr Brocklesby) mentioned a respectable gentleman who became
extremely penurious near the close of his life. Johnson said, "There must
have been a degree of madness about him." "Not at all, Sir, (said Dr.
B) his judgement was entire. Unluckily, however, he mentioned that
although he had a fortune of £27,000, he denied himself many comforts
from an apprehension he could not afford them."

James Boswell: *The Life of Samuel Johnson*

Never bear more than one trouble at a time; some bear three kinds – all
they have ever had, all they have now, and all they expect to have.

Lord Avebury

ART

There is as much healing power in a Beethoven sonata or a painting by
Constable as in the excerpts found in the Bible.

G. B. Shaw: *Days with Bernard Shaw*

ASSURANCE

What a happiness, what a joy it is to be quite sure that there is a God.
Not anything built up by mere human reasoning, no clever or subtle
hypothesis, nothing particularly French or German or English but
something as infinitely more real than the air around us, and the pollen
of flowers, and the flight of the birds, and the trials and troubles and the

needs of our little lives stimulated and enriched by the lives of creatures so different from ourselves, touching us continually all round; and the fundamental assurance is not simply one of variety or even of richness. It is an assurance accompanying and crowning all such sense of variety, of a reality, of the reality, one and harmonious, strong and self sufficing, of God.

> **Baron Friedrich Von Hugel:** the last paragraph dictated for his unfinished book, *The Reality of God*

ATONEMENT

What is the atonement of Christ? It is himself. It is the inherent everlasting mercy of God made apparent to human eyes and ears. The everlasting love was found in our Lord's life and death. It shows that God forgives because he loves to forgive. He works by smiles if possible; if not by frowns. Pain is only a means of enforcing love.

> **David Livingstone:** quoted by C.F. Andrews in *Christ in the Silence*

AWARENESS

Which only shows, yet once more, how right the Buddha was in classing unawareness and stupidity among the deadly sins.

> **Aldous Huxley:** *Ends and Means*

The Father has put us into the world not to walk through it with lowered eyes, but to search for him through things, events, people. Everything must reveal God to us.

> **Abbe Michel Quoist:** *Prayers of Life*

I wish to make people aware so they do not squander and dissipate their lives! The aristocrats assume that there is always a mass of men lost. But they hide the fact, they live withdrawn and behave as though these many, many men did not exist. That is what is Godless in the superiority of the aristocrats; in order to have things their own way they do not even make people aware.

> **Soren Kierkegaard**

BACKSLIDING

Twas hard work, I say, to offer to look him in the face against whom I had so vilely sinned! And indeed I have found it as difficult to come to God by prayer after backsliding from him as to do any other thing.

John Bunyan: *Grace Abounding*

BEAUTY

Beauty is truth, truth beauty – that is all
Ye know on earth and all ye need to know.

Keats: *Ode on a Grecian Urn*

A thing of beauty is a joy forever:
Its loveliness increases; it will never
Pass into nothingness; but still will keep
A bower quiet for us and a sleep
Full of sweet dreams and health and quiet dreaming.

Keats: *Endymion*

Thanks to the human heart by which we live,
Thanks to its tenderness, its joys and fears,
To me the meanest flower that blows can give
Thoughts that do often lie too deep for tears.

Wordsworth: *Intimations of Immortality*

Never lose an opportunity to see anything beautiful. Beauty is God's handwriting.

Charles Kingsley

One becomes amazingly receptive after two years dearth of the pure elements of earth. What it means to have around the hills and meadows, fields and forests after prison grills and walls: the scent of flowers instead of smoke and steam from damp clothing; bird chorus instead of the grind of machinery day and night – that cannot be put into words.

From pamphlet *In Prison - Yet Free* by **Eva Herman**,
a Quaker imprisoned 1943-45 by Nazis for befriending Jews.

I heard a hospital chairman say: 'I've seen a patient's life on the wobble, when bacteriology could do no more, and help came from a bowl of roses.' That bowl of roses was symbolic. It represented those tender graces, those healing kindnesses, which mean so much to those that are ill and in pain.

Philip Inman: *No Going Back*

Beauty is a token fallen from heaven to earth in order to remind us of the ideal world.

Henri Frederic Amiel: *Journal*

Beauty, so old, so new. Too late I love thee.

St. Augustine

If I give you a rose, you cannot doubt God any more.

Tertullian

Charles Kingsley, in his last illness was overheard saying to himself, "How beautiful God is.
I love all beauteous things
I seek and adore them
God hath no better praise
And man in his hasty days
Is honoured for them"

Robert Bridges

The beautiful is that kind of good in which the soul rests without possession.

St. Thomas Aquinas: quoted by
Paul Tillich: *History of Christian Thought*

For he who would proceed aright in this manner should begin in youth to visit beautiful forms; and first, if he be guided by his instructor aright, to love one such form only – out of that he should create fair thoughts; and soon he will of himself perceive that the beauty of one form is akin to the beauty of another and that beauty in every form is one and the same.

Plato: quoted by Rollo May in *The Courage to Create*

Belief

It is in the light of our beliefs about the ultimate nature of reality that we formulate our conception of right and wrong; and it is in the light of our conceptions of right and wrong that we frame our conduct, not only in the relations of private life, but also in the sphere of politics and economics.

Aldous Huxley: *Ends and Means*

Belief consists in accepting the affirmations of the soul; unbelief in denying them.

Emerson

To believe means to endure tension questions unsolved.

John Henry Newman, quoted by Ida Gorres

Belief is no adequate substitute for inner experience, and where this is absent even a strong faith which comes miraculously as a gift of grace may depart equally miraculously. People call faith the true religious experience but they do not stop to think that actually it is a secondary phenomenon arising from the fact that something happened to us in the first place which instilled 'piotos' into us – that is, trust and loyalty etc.

Carl Jung: *The Undiscovered Self*

Bible

Before, as I walked about on my hunting, or for viewing the country, the anguish of my soul at my condition would break out upon me on a sudden, and my very heart would die within me to think of the woods, the mountains, the deserts I was in; and how I was a prisoner locked up with the eternal bars and bolts of the ocean, in an uninhabited wilderness, without redemption.

But I began to exercise myself with new thoughts. I daily read the Word of God, and applied all the comforts of it to my present state. One morning, being very sad, I opened the Bible on these words, "I will never leave thee, nor forsake thee!" Immediately it occurred to me that these words were to me. Why else should they be directed in such a manner, just at the moment when I was mourning over my condition, as one forsaken of God and Man? "Well then," said I, "If God does not forsake me, of what ill consequence can it be, or what matters it that the world should all forsake me, seeing, on the other hand, if I had all the world and should lose the favour and blessing of God, there would be no comparison in the loss?"

I never opened my Bible or shut it, but my very soul within me blessed God for directing my friend in England, without any order of mine, to pack it among my goods, and for assisting me afterwards to save it out of the wreck of the ship.

Daniel Defoe: *Robinson Crusoe*

I have found words for my inmost thoughts, songs for my joy, utterances for my hidden griefs, and pleadings for my shame and feebleness.

Samuel Taylor Coleridge: *Confessions of an Enquiring Spirit.*

Whereof one day, when I was in meeting of God's people, full of sadness and terror (for my fears again were strong upon me) and as I was now thinking, my soul was never the better, but my case most sad and fearful, these words did with great power suddenly break in on me: my grace is sufficient for thee, my grace is sufficient for thee, my grace is sufficient for thee, three times together and oh, methought that every word was a mighty word unto me, as "my" and "grace" and "sufficient" and "for thee". They were then and sometimes still are far bigger than others be.

John Bunyan: *Grace Abounding*

Professor T.H. Huxley had such men in mind in his great panegyric on the Bible, when, after bidding us consider that, "This book has been woven into the life of all that is best and noblest in English history", he concludes, "And finally that it forbids the veriest hind who never left his village, to be ignorant of the existence of other countries and other civilisations in the world, and of a great past stretching back to the furthest limits of the oldest nations in the world. By the study of what other book could children be so humanised and made to feel that each figure in that vast historical procession, fills, like themselves, but a momentary space in the intervals between two eternities, and earns the blessings or the curses of all time according to its efforts to do good and hate evil, even as they are also earning their payment for their work.

T. H. Huxley *Collected Essays Volume 3, Science and Education*, quoted by Victor Murray, *Education into Religion*

Holy scripture is a sweet scented herb and the more you rub it the more it emits its fragrance.

Martin Luther

I will spread out before thee the pleasant fields of Holy Scripture, that with an enlarged heart thou mayest begin to run the way of my commandments.

Thomas A Kempis

I stand with the Quaker, John Woolman, in believing that there is more light waiting to break out of His word.

John J. Vincent

The Word did it all, I left it to the Word.

Martin Luther

The words of St Paul are not dead words; they are living creatures and have hands and feet.

Martin Luther: quoted in *Ways: Letters of St. Paul*

The Bible is the greatest sermon in the world.

P.T. Forsyth *Positive Preaching and the Modern World*
(See entry on Tolstoy under **Inspiration**)

Books

A good book is the precious lifeblood of a master spirit, embalmed and treasured up on purpose to a life beyond life.

John Milton: *Areopagitica*

CALL OF GOD

Marmaduke Stevenson: "In the beginning of the year 1653, I was at the plough in the East part of Old England near the place where my outward being was and as I walked after the plough I was filled with the love and presence of the living God, which did ravish my heart when I felt it, for it did increase and abound in me like a living stream, so did the life and love of God run through me like precious ointment giving a pleasant smell which made me to stand still. And as I stood a little still, with my heart and mind stayed upon the Lord, the word of the Lord came to me in a still small voice, which I did hear perfectly saying to me in the secret of my heart and conscience, "I have ordained thee a prophet unto the nations" and at the hearing of the word of the Lord I was put to a stand, seeing that I was but a child for such a weighty matter." But since disobedience was out of the question, Marmaduke Stevenson put aside his plough and sailed for the Barbadoes, eventually reaching Massachusetts where he paid for his faith with his life.

Florence Higham *Faith of our Fathers*

CHANGE

Change is the nursery of music, joy, life, and eternity. Great dividing line in Europe, in fact in the entire world, is not the line between right and left. All of us who grew up in the intellectual atmosphere of the twenties were sincerely convinced that people who were politically to the left of the middle acted under a moral incentive. Indeed, as I have said, in most radicals there had been during the early post-war period, underneath it all, a love of justice and a compassion for the multitude. Conversely, it was held that people were conservative out of material motives for conservatism. No matter how much some of them were able to deceive themselves in this respect, the Nazi years taught us a lesson. It happened, not infrequently, that you met a friend whom you had known for years as a "staunch liberal" and he turned out to be eagerly ready for any compromise that would save his skin. On the other hand, we saw people whom we had disdained as reactionaries go to the concentration camps and to the gallows. In the beginning it seemed confusing. But gradually it became clearer, and it was obvious that the only thing that counts in this world is the strength of moral conviction.

Karl Stern: *The Pillar of Fire*

CHANGED LIFE

For the radical and permanent transformation of personality only
one effective method has been discovered – that of the mystics. It is a
difficult method demanding from those who undertake it a great deal
more patience, resolution, self-abnegation and awareness than most
people are prepared to give.

Aldous Huxley: *Grey Eminence*

Society can never be greatly improved until such time as most of its
members choose to become theocentric saints.

Aldous Huxley: *Grey Eminence*

The only conceivable way of bringing about a reconstruction of our
world is first of all to become new men under the old circumstances.

Albert Schweitzer

"I felt I did trust in Christ, Christ alone for salvation; and an assurance
was given me that he had taken away my sins, even mine and saved me
from the law of sin and death." Wesley at once began to pray earnestly
for his enemies and publicly testified to all present what he now felt.

John Wesley: John Telford, *Life of John Wesley*

Robinson wrote to Bolivar. "Only understand that to make a new
republic one must first make a new people."

Samuel Robinson attributed by J. B. Trend: *Bolivar and the
Independence of Spanish America*

A believer is not very holy if he is not very kind.

Andrew Bonar: *Heavenly Springs*

I think it is a very poor kind of holiness that does not make us care for
others.

Andrew Bonar: *Heavenly Springs*

H. H. Kramer quotes a saying of **J. C. Blumhardt:** "Every Christian
needs two conversions: first to Christ and then to the world".

Reverend Daniel Jenkins: *Beyond Religion*

CHARITY

It is for your love alone that men will pardon you for the bread you give to them.

St. Vincent de Paul *to* his novices. Quoted in
Congregational Prayer Fellowship Handbook 1971

CHEERFULNESS

Constant cheerfulness is the sure sign of a wise mind.

Montaigne

CHRIST

He comes to us as One unknown, without a name, as of old, by the lake side, He came to those men who knew Him not. He speaks to us the same word: "Follow thou me!" and sets us to the tasks which He has to fulfill for our time. He commands. And to those who obey Him, whether they be wise or simple, He will reveal Himself in the toils, the conflicts, the sufferings which they shall pass through in His fellowship.
The earth, the sea and the air

Albert Schweitzer: *The Quest of the Historical Jesus*

Any one who ventures to look the historical Jesus straight in the face and to listen for what he has to teach him in his powerful sayings, soon ceases to ask what this strange seeming Jesus can still be to him. He learns to know him as one who claims authority over him.

Albert Schweitzer: *The Quest of the Historical Jesus*

Not the historical Jesus but the spirit which goes forth from him and in the spirits of men strives for new influence and rule, is that which overcomes the world.

Albert Schweitzer: *The Quest of the Historical Jesus*

Jesus means something to our world because a mighty spiritual force streams forth from him and flows through our time also. This fact can neither be confirmed nor shaken nor confirmed by any historical discovery. It is the solid foundation of Christianity.

Albert Schweitzer: *The Quest of the Historical Jesus* quoted by Oldham: *Life is Commitment*

Schweitzer also asserts: "To me, however, Jesus remains what he was. Not for a single minute have I had to struggle for my conviction that in Him is the supreme spiritual and religious authority."

Albert Schweitzer: *The Quest of the Historical Jesus* quoted by Oldham: *Life is Commitment*

To one of his officers on his island prison: "I am a great failure; but Jesus the carpenter of Nazareth is a world conqueror."

Napoleon; Dickie: *Fellowship of Youth*

When we have truly found Christ we can go through the world alone.

Andrew A. Bonar: *Heavenly Springs*

If Christ is a man, and only a man I say
That of all mankind I will cleave to him
And to him I will cleave always
If Jesus Christ is a God
And the only God I swear
I will follow him through heaven and hell
The earth, the sea and the air.
Christ is the stooping down of God, the arm of God on which we can lean; the heart of God of which we can feel the sympathy; the eye of God of which we can bear the glance; the voice of God which is music, melody and peace.

Richard Watson Gilder

He who prayed for the fickle Peter still lives to strengthen us against temptation to keep our faith from failing. The work which Jesus did on earth goes on in the eternal order. He is active now in bringing into the world the fruits of his redeeming love, and his death and resurrection have permanently changed the balance of spiritual forces in the universe.

Gordon S. Wakefield: *The Life of the Spirit Today*

Real confrontation, decision and action in the areas of modern life which matter at the moment occur where people open themselves to the real issues involved. For the Christian one of the elements in every situation is the living Christ.

John Vincent: *Here I Stand*

...For from the hour of my birth, to my death on the cross; I was not without suffering or grief. I suffered great want of things temporal. I often heard many complaints... etc.

Thomas A Kempis: *Imitation of Christ Book 4 (13)*

CHRIST AND WORLD ISSUES

I doubt whether Christ should be brought into the technical details of policy towards Germany, such as dismantling, because I do not pretend to know what his views would have been on this issue.

Lord Vansittart: *letter to the Manchester Guardian* Autumn 1949

CHRISTIANITY

Christianity is eternity in the midst of time.

Adolf Von Harnack

The truth of Christianity cannot be proved to the man in the street till he come off the street by owning its power.

P. T. Forsyth: *Cruciality of the Cross.*

Christianity is not primarily demand but fulfilment.

J. H. Oldam: *Life is Commitment*

Christianity is avowedly the most materialistic of all religions ... If we allow the spiritual and the physical to become separated, the unity of man's life is broken; the material world, with all man's economic activity becomes a happy hunting ground for uncurbed acquisitiveness and religion becomes a refined occupation for the leisure of the mystical. It is in the sacramental view of the universe, both of its material and of its spiritual elements, that there is given hope of making human both politics and economics and of making effectual both faith and love.

William Temple: *Nature, Man and God.*
Quoted by J. H. Oldham *Life is Commitment*

CHRISTIAN BELIEF

Christian faith is a risk. But unbelief is no less a risk. It is the risk of missing the best that life can offer. Scepticism may close the door to renovating experience. We may suffer ineffable loss by remaining blind to truths which we lack the daring to apprehend or to goodness and beauty which we are too dull to perceive. Life is a risk every way. It is as we said in the first lecture - decision, commitment, adventure.

J.H. Oldham: *Life is Commitment*

Scepticism is very often the basis for a doctrine of revelation.

Paul Tillich: *History of Christian Thought*

CHRISTMAS

O perfect love, out passing sight,
O love beyond our ken,
Come down through all the world tonight
And heal the hearts of men.

Laurence Housman

Bid our peace increase
Thou that madest morn;
Bid oppression cease;
Bid the night be peace,
Bid the day be borne.
As this night was bright,
With thy cradle ray
Very light of light,

From the wild world's night
To thy perfect day.

Algernon Swinburne

The people thronged to Bethlehem
The people came
They came to laugh to talk to stare,
They came to sign the census there;
The people came
I too have come to Bethlehem,
I too have come;
I came a Saviour to adore
Of grace and love he has great store:
I, too, have come.

Dorothy M. Gotch

Still to the lowly soul,
He doth himself impart,
And for his cradle and his throne,
Chooseth the pure in heart.

John Keble: *Blest are the pure in heart*

When God gave music to the world it was not in some theory of
counterpoint and harmony; he dressed a song in feathers and sat it on
a tree. When God gave love to the world it was not in some thesis on
the emotions; He implanted it in a mother's heart. When God gave
Himself to the world it was not in some new piece of theology. He
wrapped a babe in swaddling clothes and laid him in a manger. 'Let us
go, even unto Bethlehem and see this thing which is come to pass.'
Unattributed

There is nothing I can give you which you have not; but there is much
that, while I cannot give, you can take. No heaven can come to us unless
our hearts find rest in it today. No peace lies in the future which is not
hidden in the present instant. Take peace. The gloom of this world is
but a shadow; behind it, yet within reach, is joy. Take joy and so at this
Christmastime I greet you with the prayer that for you day break and
the shadows flee away.

Don Giovanni

CHURCH

The ultimate criterion to distinguish a false or moribund church from a true and living church is the power of Jesus Christ himself.

John Mackay: *God's Order*

The church is a siding into which Christianity has been shunted to keep it out of the traffic on the main line. Every now and then the driver of the shunted train tries to get it going again (while his mates sit around drinking) and when he is feeling particularly bold he blows the whistle.

Pierre Ceresole

'Sire, it is in truth the lot of the Church of God, in whose name I speak, to suffer blows and not to return them. Yet I also take leave to remind you that she is an anvil which has employed many hammers.'

Addressed by Beza to the King of Navarre after the massacre of Vassey. **J.S. Whale:** *The Protestant Tradition*

The Church is not a community of escape. It is a community of expectancy.

Max Warren: *The Christian Mission*

The Church is the fellowship of the dead to themselves and alive for Christ.

Nels Ferré: in *Christ and the Christian*; quoted by William Barclay: *Plain Man Looks at the Beatitudes*

Wherever you see this word preached, believed, confessed and acted on, do not doubt that there must be a true ecclesia sancta catholica...for God's word does not go away empty.

Martin Luther quoted by Lesslie Newbigin: *The Household of God*

Wherever we see the word of God sincerely preached and heard, wherever we see the sacraments administered according to the institution of Christ, there we cannot have any doubt that the Church of God has some existence, since his promise cannot fail, 'Where two or three are gathered together in my name, there am I in the midst.'

Calvin: *Institution IV 1.9* quoted by Lesslie Newbigin: *The Household of God*

The Protestant idea of a church, expressed in the Augsburg Confession, and in very similar terms in the Thirty Nine Articles (nineteenth article) is that the visible church is a congregation of faithful or believing men, "In which the pure Word of God is preached and the sacraments administered according to Christ's ordinance in all those things that of necessity are requisite to the same."

Henry Wace: *Principles of the Reformation*

The Church is her true self only when she exists for humanity.

Dietrich Bonhoeffer

The Church exists by mission, just as a fire exists by burning.

Emil Brunner

St. Augustine, somewhere, has a phrase about the church of his day, as, like a frost bound tree, seeming dead, but waiting for the summer. Sacred Trinity had every sign of being dead but waiting for nothing.

Canon Peter Green quoted by Rev. H. E. Sheen

We must say bluntly that when the church ceases to be a mission, then she ceases to have any right to the titles by which she is adorned in the New Testament.

Lesslie Newbigin, quoted by Richard G Jones,
Anthony J Wesson *Towards a Radical Church*

The Church is nothing but a section of humanity in which Christ has really taken form.

Dietrich Bonhoeffer, quoted by J. V. Taylor *The Go-between God*

There can be no Word of God without the people of God.

Martin Luther, quoted by The Reverend Dr. Colin Morris:
The Word and the Words

CIVILISATION

(During the 30 Years War)...The habit of committing atrocities had developed a general taste for atrocities. With cruelty, as with lust, avarice, gluttony and the love of power: l'appetit vien en mangeant.

Hence the importance of preserving at any cost the unreasoned tradition of civilised conduct, the social convention of ordinary decency. Destroy these and immediately large numbers of men and women, discovering within themselves no obvious reasons why they should not behave like devils, do behave like devils and go on doing so until such time as they physically destroy themselves, or grow weary of the strain and uncertainty of diabolic life, or else, for whatever providential reason, discover deep in their own souls the hidden springs of compassion, the potential goodness, latent even in the worst of men and by the best, fully actualised in the superhuman splendour of saintliness.

Aldous Huxley: *Grey Eminence*

COMMITTEES

I grant you that the 47 men who produced the Authorised Version worked in the main upon Tyndale's version, taking that for their basis...But when Tyndale has been granted, you have yet to face the miracle that forty seven men – not one of them known outside this performance, for any superlative talent – sat in committee, and almost consistently over a vast extent of work – improved what genius had done. I give you the word of an old committeeman that this is not the way of committees.

Sir Arthur Quiller Couch: *The Art of Writing*

COMMITMENT (see Self-surrender)

Do you really have feelings any longer for anybody or anything except your self – or even that? Without the strength of a personal commitment, your experience of others is most aesthetic etc.

Dag Hammersjkold: *Markings*

Hold to Christ and for the rest be uncommitted.

Herbert Butterfield

CONCENTRATION

One of the busiest of city dentists was once asked how he managed to do his work with such calm efficiency when he knew that the adjoining

room was crowded with people awaiting him. His reply was that for
him only one patient existed.

Unattributed

CONCISENESS

If there be a man upon earth tormented by the cursed desire to get a
whole book into a page, a whole page into a phrase and this phrase into
a word – that man is myself.

Joseph Joubert

It is the thought that must be polished...Once it is perfected its
expression will drop from the pen as lucid and shining as a drop of
water.

Joseph Joubert

CONGREGATIONALISM

If the danger of parochialism is less, the danger of congregationalism
is great. It is here that our sense of national responsibility is in greater
danger and with it, perhaps, our claim to genuine catholicity, for we
cease to be Christ's Holy Catholic Church in the place and become a
mere eclectic enclave of people who happen to like the type of service or
the character of the preaching.

Frank Bennet C of E (sic):
Laodicea in the Twentieth Century

Our government is through the synod, composed of ministers and
deputies from each congregation. The synod has final authority over
every phase of our corporate thought or branch of corporate work,
every congregation or Board of Administration or portion of property.
The synod may be regarded as a representative body suitable to the
democratic character of a church which calls itself 'unitas fratrum'.
But really, it seeks to stand for something higher still, and comes down
from early days before the word 'democratic' enjoyed the high reputation
it has today. There were days when our forefathers were greatly
exercised in their minds over the question of government. They were
anxiously asking themselves who should be appointed to the position
of 'Chief Elder', to use the title then employed. Who was to be the chief

authority in the church? And it flashed on their minds that no human being was fitted or could be called to that position. For that position was already filled by Christ himself – Christ was the chief elder of the church. Let every gathering and every administrative or governing function be placed under Christ's direction. And the Synod was meant to be the body of Christians meeting to receive the direction of the true head of the Church. To use a theological term, the Synod was to be the organ of a Christocracy.

Rt. Rev. C. H. Shawe D.D. *The Moravian Church and What it Stands For.*

CONSCIENCE

His gain is loss, for he that wrongs a friend
Wrongs himself more, and ever bears about
A silent court of justice in his breast
Himself the judge and jury, and himself
The prisoner at the bar, ever condemned.

Alfred Lord Tennyson: *Sea Dreams*

If it had power as it has manifest authority it would rule the world.

Bishop Butler

If we are not in black books with our conscience we may whistle o'er the lave o't whoever is pleased or grumpy. (i.e. whistle over the rest of it – the title of a song by Robert Burns).

From a letter by **David Livingstone** to Robert Moffat 4th May(?) 1849

Conscience with Isaiah is not what it is with so much religion of today, a cul-de-sac in which the Lord chases a man and shuts him up to himself, but it is a thoroughfare by which the Lord drives the man out upon the world and its manifold need of him.

George Adam Smith *Book of Isaiah*

The good conscience is an invention of the devil.

Albert Schweitzer

My heart is abundantly satisfied that I cannot subscribe without sinning against God, wronging my own conscience and giving offence to the people of God. Well thou my soul, since thou art thus resolved, prepare thyself for suffering and glory that thou art counted worthy to suffer for the name of Christ.

Oliver Heywood

Albert Schweitzer is quite right to say that, "the good conscience is an invention of the devil."

Joseph Fletcher: *Situation Ethics* referencing
J. A. Davidson *A New Look at Morals*

CONSOLATION

If thou canst not contemplate high and heavenly things; rest in the passion of Christ; and dwell gladly in his sacred wounds. For if thou fly devoutly to the wounds, and precious marks of Jesus; thou shalt feel great comfort in tribulation; thou wilt not much care for the slights of men; and wilt easily bear words of detraction.

Thomas A Kempis: *Imitation of Christ*

CONTENTMENT

…And though by reason of the many losses he sustained by imprisonment and spoil, of his chargeable sickness, etc., his earthly treasure swelled not to excess, he always had sufficient to live decently and credibly; And with that he had the greatest of all treasures, which is content.

Of John Bunyan: *Grace Abounding*

Art thou poor yet hast thou golden slumbers?
O sweet content!

Thomas Dekker: *Sweet Content*

Contentment consists not in great wealth but in few wants.

Epictetus

One of the chief reasons for discontent is that people do not find the right niche in the world.

John Rowland: *Sir Alexander Fleming: The Penicillin Man*

CONVERSION

It is to be observed that this suddenness of change or flash of conviction is by no means of the essence of true conversion, and it is to be no more demanded in ourselves or others than such a light from heaven as shone round St. Paul and cast him to the ground. Etc.

William Law: *Christian Regeneration Works*

Christianity affords and teaches salvation by the conversion of the will; but humanism by the emancipation of the spirit.

Henri Frederic Amiel: *Journal* 7/4/51

By personal conversion, I mean a sustained act of will whereby someone chooses to follow the way of Jesus – a decision whose long-term consequence is a fundamental character change. It is the decision to make the priorities of Jesus his own and to derive the power source of his life from that which sustained Jesus. Etc

The Reverend Dr. Colin Morris: *The Hammer of the Lord*

In my view, conversion does not mean adding an extra dimension – the religious – to all other dimensions of our existence, but the unsnarling of the tangled threads of our lives, so that, by an act of the will, we bring our priorities into line with these of Jesus and derive the power for living from the same sources as that from which Jesus drew his. Hence, when someone approaches me with the light of religious fervour in his eyes and assures me joyously that he has been converted, I do not want to know what effect this experience has had upon his church-going or prayer life, but how it has manifested itself on the pressure points of his life – in his attitudes to sex, money, power, race, politics, etc. etc.

The Reverend Dr. Colin Morris: *The Word and the Words*

CO-OPERATION

For we are made for co-operation, like feet, like hands, like eyelids, like the rows of the upper and lower teeth. To act against one another is against human nature.

Marcus Aurelius: *Meditations*

COURAGE

Courage is not the absence of despair; it is rather the capacity to move ahead in spite of despair.

Rollo May: *Courage to Create*

And again -
Courage is not the opposite of despair. Kierkegaard and Nietsche and Camus and Sartre have proclaimed that courage is the absence of despair; it is rather the capacity to move ahead in spite of despair.

Rollo May: *Courage to Create*

Courage is not a virtue or value amongst other personal values like love or fidelity. It is the foundation that underlies and gives reality to all other virtues and personal values. Without courage love pales into mere dependency! (??) Without courage our fidelity becomes conformism.

Rollo May: Courage to Create

COURTESY

Whence St. Francis, seeing so much courtesy and goodwill in him, said, "Know most dearly beloved brother, that courtesy is one of the properties of God, who gives his sun and rain to the just and the unjust by courtesy; and courtesy is the sister of charity, by which hatred is extinguished and love is cherished."

Anonymous: *Little Flowers of St Francis*

Dryden's remark about Jeremy Collier, "I will not say, 'the zeal of God's house has eaten him up' but I am sure it has devoured some part of his good manners and civility."

Quoted by **Harry Emerson Fosdick:** *The Living of These Days*

COVETOUSNESS

A dirty brown penny held near enough to the eye can blot out the sun.

H. F. Lovell Cocks M.A. D.D.

CREATION

They (the creation stories of Genesis) are a recasting of ancient myths of creation, paradise and the fall of man, produced at a comparatively late stage in the history of Israel and reflecting a highly developed understanding of a God who had entered into personal dealings with his people, through the covenant and the law...They (these stories) are imaginative expressions of permanent realities with which other religions have also tried in their own way to grapple but now illumined and given meaning by the knowledge of God's purpose made known in his covenant with Israel.

Reverend Daniel Jenkins: *Christian Belief in God*

CREEDS

In answer to this, I must in all honesty set my longstanding and assured conviction that creedal subscription to ancient confessions of faith is a practice dangerous to the integrity of the individual conscience.

Harry Emerson Fosdick: *The Living of These Days*

CROSS

The cross has always been a window into the heart of God, the supreme means of awakening men to the overwhelming and humbling reality of God's amazing love. And without it, faith could only have made its home in the shadows of half knowledge and dim guesses. In its light, the pattern of sin and holiness, of grossness and purity stand out in the clearest relief and we know both for what they are. That is why the Cross has always at one and the same time convinced men of sin and convinced them of the reality of forgiveness, has both diagnosed the disease and provided the remedy.

B. C. Plowright: *Everyman Prays*

When Portuguese traders, following the trail of the great explorer, Vasco da Gama, settled on the south coast of China, they built a massive cathedral on a hillcrest overlooking the harbour. But a violent typhoon proved too severe, and three centuries ago the great building fell, all except the front wall. The ponderous façade has stood as an enduring monument while high on its triangular top, clean cut against the sky and defying rain, lightning and typhoon is a great bronze cross. When Sir John Bowring, then governor of Hong Kong visited Macao in 1825 he was so impressed with the scene that he wrote the hymn beginning:

In the cross of Christ I glory
Towering o'er the wrecks of time
All the light of sacred story
Gathers round its head sublime.

The buildings of the ancient cathedral are forgotten but the cross they reared in memory of the crucified remains. China has seen stupendous changes. Old institutions have crumbled and dynasties disappeared. But the cross still stands.

S. W. Zwemer: from *World Christian Digest* April 1952

Thus Lord, I must gather my body, my heart, my spirit and stretch myself at full length on the cross of the present moment. I haven't the right to choose the wood of my passion. The cross is ready to my measure.

Abbe Michel Quoist: *Prayers of Life*

If thou carry the cross cheerfully, it will carry thee, and lead thee to the desired end, namely where there is an end to suffering, though here there shall be none.

Thomas A Kempis: *The Imitation of Christ*

CULTURE

The value of culture is its effect on character. It avails nothing unless it ennobles and strengthens that. Its use is for life. Its aim is not beauty but goodness.

W. Somerset Maugham: *The Summing Up*

DEATH

But when the morn came dim and sad
And chill with early showers
Her quiet eyelids closed – she had
Another morn than ours

Thomas Hood: *The Death Bed*

Into the hand that made the rose
Shall I with shuddering fall?

George Meredith

Now death was lovely and beautiful in my sight, for I saw we shall never
live indeed till we be gone to the other side.

John Bunyan: *Grace Abounding*

Now was I got on high, I saw myself within the arms of grace and
mercy; and though I was afraid before to think of a dying, yet now I
cried, let me die. Now death was lovely and beautiful in my sight, for I
saw we shall never live indeed till we be gone to the other world.

John Bunyan: *Grace Abounding*

It is not growing like a tree
In bulk doth make a man better be;
Or standing long an oak, three hundred year
To fall at last, dry bald and sere;
A lily of a day
Is fairer far in May
Although it fall and die that night –
It was the plant and flower of light.
In small proportions we just beauties see
And in short measures life may perfect be.

Ben Jonson

In the hour of death, after this life's whim,
When the heart beats low and the eyes grow dim
And pain has exhausted every limb -
The lover of the Lord shall trust in him.

When the will has forgotten the lifelong aim,
And the mind can only disgrace its fame,
And a man is uncertain of his own name -
The power of the Lord shall fill this frame.

IBRA Handbook 1957

He then made mention of his end which he believed was near; and
signified that though he was sensible of many imperfections in the
course of his life, yet his experience of the power of truth and of the love
and goodness of God from time to time, even till now, was such that on
leaving this life he had no doubt he should enter one more happy.

John Woolman: *Journal*

Said of his father
Away! We know that tears are vain,
That death nor heeds nor hears distress;
Will this unteach us to complain?
Or make one mourner weep the less?
And thou who tell'st me to forget,
Thy looks are wan, thine eyes are wet.

Lord Byron: *Oh! Snatch'd Away in Beauty's Bloom*
(See J. Singleton *Epilogues for Youth*)

So shalt thou feed on death, that feed on men,
And death, once dead, there's no more dying then

William Shakespeare: *Sonnet 146*

He never wasted a leaf on a tree. Do you think he will squander souls?

Rudyard Kipling

Death is a gate on the skyline.

Mary Webb

Life is eternal and love is immortal and death is only an horizon, and an
horizon is nothing save the limit of our sight.

Bishop Brent

Thou madest death and lo, Thy foot is on
the skull that thou hast made.

Alfred Lord Tennyson: *In Memoriam*

We asked him for life, but thou hast given him even eternal life.

Anon: (see Psalm 21 v 4)

...As the African says to the soul of his dying friend, "Come back, this is
your home".

Olwyn Campbell: *Mary Kingsley*

Departure is really only a transfer from one sphere of service to
another, by the master who knows what he is doing and never errs. If
we understand at least something of our task here, we shall not resent
the change of duties but co-operate right up to the threshold of this
sovereign act of his translation. In that meek submission, we shall enter
into our inheritance.

Geoffrey T. Bull: *World Christian Digest*,
Sept. 1959 from the book *God Holds the Key*

This is the end - for me the beginning of life.

Dietrich Bonhoeffer: last words before he was hanged,
April 1945, in a Nazi Extermination Camp.

St. Theresa of Lisieux, on her death bed murmured, "I am not dying, I
am entering into life."

Abbe Michel Quoist: *Prayers of Life*

Death is but the side of life that is turned from us.

Rainer Maria Rilke; quoted by Neville Ward, *Use of Praying*

DECISION

Decision is a risk rooted in the courage of being free.

Paul Tillich: *Systematic Theology* Vol.1.
Quoted by J. Fletcher in *Situation Ethics*

DEDICATION

Once, I answered yes to someone – or something. And from that hour I was certain that existence was meaningful and that therefore, my life in self-surrender has a goal.

Dag Hammarskjold: *Markings* Whit Sunday 1961

DEMOCRACY

The vice or imperfection of men therefore renders it safer and more tolerable for government to be in the hands of many, that they may afford each other mutual admonition and assistance and that if any one abrogate to himself more than his right, the many may act as censors and masters to restrain his ambition.

John Calvin: *Institutes of the Christian Religion Vol. 4*

DESPAIR

Man's depth would be despair but for God's deeper depth.

Christina Rossetti

Wars with their noise affright us, when they cease,
We are worse in peace:-
What then remains, but that we still should cry
For being born, or being born to die

Lord Bacon: *Life*

Human life begins on the far side of despair.

Jean-Paul Sartre: Orestes in *The Flies*

DETACHMENT

The world is possessed by those who are not possessed by it.

Dr. Inge

Poverty is naught to have and nothing to desire; but all things to possess in the spirit of liberty.

Jacopone Da Tobi; *quoted in* J.R.H. Moorman's
St Francis of Assisi

Regard not much who is for thee or against thee: but see thou well to this, that God be with thee in everything.

T. A. Kempis: *Imitation of Christ* Book 2

DETERMINISM, ETC. FREE WILL

Any given event in any part of the universe has as its determining conditions all previous and contemporary events in all parts of the universe. Those, however, who make it their business to investigate the causes of what goes on around them habitually ignore the overwhelming majority of contemporary and antecedent happenings. In each particular case, they insist, only a very few of the determining conditions are of practical significance.

Aldous Huxley: *Grey Eminence*

The psychoanalytical contention that all the divagations of the sub-conscious carry a deep passional significance cannot be made to fit the facts. One has only to observe oneself and others to observe that we are no more exclusively the servants of our passions and our biological urges than we are exclusively rational. We are also created possessed of a very complicated psycho-physiological machine which grinds away incessantly and in them course of its grinding throws up into consciousness selections from that indefinite number of mental permutations and combinations struck out in the course of its random functionings.

Aldous Huxley: *Grey Eminence*

All theory is against freedom of the will; all experience for it.

Dr. Johnson 1778

Occasionally one's scepticism is apt to be shaken and life assume
the proportions of a geometrical pattern, rather than the strictly
mathematical proposition which it actually is. Intellectually speaking
one knows that life is an endless series of causes and effects and that
there can be no deviation from the scientific formula, but an innate
superstition will sometimes impinge on the rigidity of rationality.
It is much easier to believe in something called fate or destiny, or a
divinity that shapes our ends rough hew them how we will, than not
to do so. But the whole discipline of straight thinking lies in resisting
the seductive comfort of superstition and the teasing coquetry of
coincidence.

Ethel Mannin: *Confessions and Impressions*

As I pointed out, all the obvious arguments are arguments for
determinism and it is exceedingly difficult to discover any purely
rational grounds for believing in freedom. Nevertheless, in spite of those
arguments, most of us are convinced that we are free.

C. E. Joad: *Guide to Philosophy*

To my fellow men – a heart of love
To my God – a heart of flame
To myself – a heart of steel.

St. Augustine

He complacently assumed that he was a man without prejudices, not
realising that this assumption was blatant prejudice.
Anatole France: *Le Crime de Sylvestre Bonnard* quoted by J. S. Whale in
The Protestant Tradition

Is it a mere coincidence that modern thought has come to terms with
Einstein's relativity theory and with ideas about the structure of the
atom which lead us away from determinism and visual representation?
Carl Jung: *Modern Man in Search of a Soul*

Difference – made by Messiah

...The Hassidic story related by Martin Buber. A Rabbi who happened

to be in Jerusalem heard the great trumpets blow, and there was a
rumour that The Messiah had come. The Rabbi opened his window,
looked around and said, "I see no change."

Karl Stern: *The Pillar of Fire*

DISCIPLINE

True discipline is the harnessing of enthusiasm.

Edgar P. Dickie: "Infantry Training" from
The Fellowship of Youth

DISTRACTION

For though we talk lightly of doing this or that to distract the mind,
it remains really as well as verbally true, that to be distracted is to be
distraught. The original Latin word does not mean relaxation, it means
being torn asunder as by wild horses. The original Greek word that
corresponds to it is used in the text which says that Judas burst asunder
in the midst.

G.K. Chesterton: "On the Prison of Jazz" from
Avowals and Denials

DOUBTS

Another experience which is but slightly less painful is to meet those
who have accepted it without ever having been able to make a decision
about it because it was never a matter of doubt. It came to them as a
matter of habit, custom or social contact. This the Gospel can never be.

Paul Tillich

"I have a hard enough time with my own doubts, without adding
somebody else's to them," said Brush in a low voice. "What are you
afraid of doubts for? There's one thing worse than doubts, that's
evasions. You're full of evasions. You don't even want to look around.
You don't give a goddam for the truths."

Thornton Wilder: *Heaven's My Destination*

Doubt is the beginning, not the end of wisdom.

Henry Ward Beecher

The act of faith is a constant dialogue with doubt.

Bishop John A. T. Robinson: *Human Face of God*

The prevalence of doubt – for all belief is founded on preliminary doubt – is the supreme characteristic of man, that which makes him distinctively human and enlightened, whereas " the ignorant doubt little, the drunkard still less, the madman never."

Prof. Susan Stebbing; quoted by A.R. Vidler in *Pragmatism and French Voluntarism*

DREAMS

"Everything of any good in the world has started with a dream," he reminded his critics.

Lord Dawson of Penn, speaking of the development of new treatment of disease which paved the way for the modern National Health Service.

DUTY

May 19th, 1780 has gone down in Connecticut history as the famous dark day. The sky was overcast at noon and by mid-afternoon had blacked over so densely, so ominously, that in that religious age, men were certain the day of judgement was at hand. The Connecticut House of Representatives was in session and as some men fell on their knees and others clamoured for an immediate adjournment, the speaker of the house got to his feet. He was a certain Colonel Davenport. He said these words. "The Day of Judgement is either approaching or it is not. If it is there is no cause for adjournment. If it is not I prefer to be found doing my duty. I wish therefore that candles may be brought."

Alistair Cooke: Home Service broadcast (*Listener*, September 9th 1948)

ENDURANCE

There must be a begynning of any great matter, but the continyewing
unto the end untill it be thoroughly finished yeldes the true glory.

Sir Francis Drake

ENTHUSIASM

When the soul shares the purpose of God, not coldly but with eager
desire, then there is a new fact in the spiritual world. A new way is
opened whereby the Lord can enter into the hearts of men.

Anon

ETERNITY

Eternity stands always fronting God;
A stern colossal image with blind eyes,
And grand dim lips, that murmurs evermore
God. God. God!

Elizabeth Barrett Browning

EVIL

...As yet I knew not that evil was nothing but the privation of good,
until at last a thing ceases altogether to be...

Augustine: *Confessions* Bk3 vii

(About evil)...'Dr. J. S. Whale puts it, 'Strictly speaking, the question is
intellectually insoluble.'

Leslie Tizzard: *Facing Life with Confidence*

EXAMPLE

The object of a Christian should be to be like Christ – never a coolie
recruiter trying to bring coolies to his master's tea garden. Preaching
your doctrine is no sacrifice at all ... It breeds an illusion in you that you
are doing your duty and that you are wise and better than your fellow

beings. But the real preaching is in being perfect, which is through meekness and love and self-dedication.

Rabindranath Tagore

A letter to C.F. Andrews from a non-Christian friend in India (in 1983) contained this passage: "You know that during the intimate friendship of these twenty years, I have never asked you anything about Christ, for your own personality has been more than sufficient for me. But now I feel you must tell how Christ lived and how he is still living in the lives of millions of people. I want you to write in simple language the story of the life of Christ – that is the most important thing you can do. There are many people in India, from high intellectuals down to the masses who take their conception of Christ from you. You are the only man who can write this book, for you have lived like him all these thirty years in India.

B. Chaturvedi and M. Sykes: *Charles Freer Andrews*

EXPERIENCE – FIRST HAND

Thus when God doth work who shall let it? And this I knew experimentally.

George Fox: *Journal*

Fellowship with God answers a thousand questions of casuistry.

Andrew A. Bonar: *Heavenly Springs*

FAITH

Faith is a bird that feels the light and sings when the dawn is still dark.

Rabindranath Tagore

We are not afraid of the future because of a bomb. We are afraid of bombs because we have no faith in the future. We no longer have faith in our ability as individuals or as nations to control our own future.

Dr Jacob Bronowski: *Listener* June 3rd, 1948

Faith is an act of consecration in which the will, the intellect and the affections all have their place. It is the resolve to live as if certain things were true, in the confident assurance that they are true, and that we shall one day find out that they are true.

Dean Inge: *Personal Religion and the Life of Devotion*

Faith, mighty faith, the promise sees
And looks to that alone;
Laughs at impossibilities
And cries: 'it shall be done'.

Charles Wesley: *Congregational Praise* 475 v4

Faith is that strange faculty by which man feels the presence of the invisible, exactly as some animals have the power of seeing in the dark. That is the difference between the Christian and the world.

F. W. Robertson

She sees the best that glimmers through the worst,
She sees the sun is hid but only for a night,
She spies the summer through the winter bud,
She tastes the fruit before the blossom falls,
She hears the lark within the songless egg,
She finds the fountain where they wailed 'mirage'.

Alfred Lord Tennyson: *The Ancient Sage*, quoted by
Harry Emerson Fosdick in *The Meaning of Faith*

"... Dean Inge's schoolboy who said, "Faith is believing what you know to be untrue'. Adds the Dean, "It is the resolution to stand or fall by the noblest hypothesis".

From **Leslie D. Weatherhead:** *Psychology, Religion and Healing*

For nothing worth proving can be proved,
Nor yet disproved; whereof be thou wise
And cling to faith beyond the forms of death.

Alfred Lord Tennyson

Faith is always a victory, not simply a weapon which wins victory.

T. H. Robinson: *Job and his Friends*

Faith is as necessary to men as wheels to a cart.

Chinese proverb

Faith is vision plus valour.

Harry Emerson Fosdick: *The Meaning of Faith*

Commenting on Hebrews, Dean Inge says the epistle makes it clear that "Faith from first to last is an activity of the soul," and of the roll of honour in Chapter II he says, "It is almost entirely of men of action, not saints and prophets."

Demaldwyn Edwards, Rev. Stalker: IBRA Reading

... Faith is best understood not as a leap into the dark but a leap into the light.

Daniel Jenkins: *The Christian Belief in God*

Faith itself is a perpetual and determined return towards God, from whom we are constantly turning away. It is not like a direct current, which has no inductive capacity; it resembles an alternating current, with successive negative and positive phases.

Paul Tournier: *Strong and Weak*

Faith is the power by which we give ourselves up to anything.
William Law: quoted by A. R. Vidler in *Christian Belief*

A living faith is not something you have to carry, but something that carries you.

J. H. Oldham: *Life is Commitment*

Faith is the assent of the whole man to the message of God.

Karl Rahner

All this is of faith – but remember what faith is; it is the acceptance on evidence of that which makes sense.

Dr. Aubrey Vine: *Chairman's Address of Congregational Church*

Faith is the power by which we commit ourselves to anything.
William Law; quoted by J Huxtable

The acceptance of the affirmative with the whole of one's being is called faith – a concept which must be freed from intellectual distortion.
Paul Tillich: *Systematic Theology* Vol.3

Fear knocked at the door; faith opened it. There was no one there.
Old English Proverb

Faith is simply the reaction of man to God's action.
Ronald Gregor Smith: *The Free Man*

All faith is passion and risk.
Paul Tillich: quoted by Ronald Gregor Smith in *The Free Man*

Faith is (in Bultman's words) the obedient submission to God's revelation in the word of proclamation.
Ronald Gregor Smith: *The Free Man*

Faith is participation in this being of Jesus (incarnation, cross and resurrection). Our relation to God is not a "religious" relationship to the highest most powerful and best being imaginable – that is not authentic transcendence – but our relation to God is a new life in "existence for others", through participation in the being of Jesus.
Dietrich Bonhoeffer: quoted by **Ronald Gregor Smith:**
The Free Man

Faith involves commitment to a decision. It is confirmed if the decision is the right one ... According to our reinterpretation faith in "God" would mean faith that comes to expression in Jesus Christ is to be made our ultimate concern.
Alistair Kee: *Way of Transcendence*

A time may come when we cannot think of any part of the faith without questioning it, and yet, far from indicating that our faith is in danger, it shows that it is very much alive.
J. Neville Ward: *Use of Praying*

Faith is knowing yet not knowing, being sure yet unsure, having certainty, yet being uncertain.

Faith is a man's convictions of what he must do, who he will be, how he will live and always in the end is shrouded in a mist.

Rex Chapman: *Prayer Fellowship Handbook* 1974

FATHER – GOD

The Muslims have 99 names for God, but among them all they have not "Our Father".

Unattributed

FEAR

They who have the fear of God in their hearts, have also love.

Treasure House of Living Religions (Sikhism)

The benefits of my education seem partly at an end, but that education had been miserably lost if I had not learned to fear something more than misfortune.

William Law when, as a non-juror, he lost his fellowship
and all the high hopes of advancement in the church.
Characters and Characteristics of William Law

Fear to do base unworthy things is valour; if they be done to us, to suffer them is valour too.

Ben Jonson

This awful fear in which the Papuan lives, Ruth – fear of spirits, of sorcerers, of enemies and of each other.

Constance Fairhill: *The Happy Island*

Fear is the catalyst of suggestion, and suggestion implants all kinds of stubborn and absurd fears in the hearts of even the most intelligent and courageous men.

Paul Tournier: *The Strong and the Weak*

... Our doubts are traitors
And make us lose the good we oft might win
By fearing to attempt.
William Shakespeare: *Measure for Measure, Act 1 Scene 4*

FELLOWSHIP

The existence of a sense of kinship and social solidarity constitutes
another reason why people tolerate the intolerable.
Aldous Huxley: *Ends and Means*

FLATTERY

... No matter, Sir, (said Johnson) they consider it as a compliment to
be talked to, as if they were wiser than they are. So true is this, Sir,
that Baxter made it a rule in every sermon that he preached, to say
something that was above the capacity of his audience.
James Boswell: *The Life of Samuel Johnson.* 1783

FOLLOWING CHRIST

But oh, how I now love those words that spake of Christ's calling as
when the Lord said to one "Follow me", and to another "Come after me";
and oh, thought I, That he would say so to me too! How gladly would I
run after him!

John Bunyan: *Grace Abounding*

You have gained battles without cannon, passed rivers without bridges,
performed forced marches without shoes, bivouacked without strong
liquors, and often without bread. Thanks for your perseverance! But
soldiers, you have done nothing for there remains much to do.
Napoleon to his troops after having secured the gates of the Alps in his
Piedmont campaign.
M. Broomhall: *Hudson Taylor: The Man who believed God*

The way of the Lord is for heroes; it is not meant for cowards.
Offer first your life and your all; then take the name of the Lord.
Gujurati Hymn

FORGIVENESS

Use every man after his desert and who should 'scape whipping? Use them after your own honour and dignity: the less they deserve, the more merit is in your bounty.

William Shakespeare: *Hamlet Act II Scene 2*

Confucius says, when answering the question, "How do you regard the principle of returning good for evil?" "What then is to be the return for good? Rather should you return justice for injustice and good for good".

Newton Flew: *Jesus and His Way*

Forgiveness is a beggar's refuge. You must pay your debts.

Newton Flew: *Jesus and His Way*

The wise man will not feel pity, for only old women and girls will be moved by tears; he will not pardon for pardon is the remission of a deserved penalty, he will be strictly and inexorably just.

Seneca, quoted by Newton Flew in *Jesus and His Way*

FORTITUDE

Philip Inman one day saw a card bearing the words "This too will pass" upon the desk of the Russian Ambassador, M. Maisky. He asked about it and received the explanation.
"I have had so many varied experiences. Sometimes the crowds have gathered outside the Embassy, booing and jeering – so angry that they would not have stopped at physical violence. Then I have looked at the words on the card and I knew it would pass. At other times the crowds have assembled cheering – when my country came into the war, for instance. Feeling perhaps a little too elated, that card would bring me back down to earth again. That too would pass.

Philip Inman: *No Going Back*

Freedom

William James in the United States compared the freedom of man in relation to the knowledge of God to the moves of a novice in chess as opposed to the counter strategy of a master of the game.

C. W. Lowry: *Trinity and Christian Devotion*

The price of liberty is the restriction of liberty.

Professor E. H. Carr

Freedom is participation in power.

Cicero (1st century)

No man is free if he fears death.

Martin Luther King

Freedom is the oxygen of soul.

Moshe Dayan: *Story of My Life*

To be free, to be able to stand up and leave everything behind – without looking back. To say "Yes".

Dag Hammerskjold: *Markings*

To become free and responsible, for this alone was man created and he who takes the way which could have been his is lost eternally.

Dag Hammerskjold: *Markings*

The Americans speak so much about freedom in their sermons. Freedom as a possession is a doubtful thing for a church; freedom must be won under the compulsion of necessity. Freedom for the church comes from the necessity of the Word of God. Otherwise it becomes arbitrariness and ends in a great many new ties. Whether the church in America is really free, I doubt.

Dietrich Bonhoeffer: *The Way to Freedom*

Friendship

The friends thou hast and their adoption tried,
Grapple them to the soul with hoops of steel
William Shakespeare: *Hamlet* Act 1 Scene 3

Now I assert that the most precious of all this world's blessing is
true friendship, which must be accounted not a worldly good but a
heavenly blessing; for it is not false fate that produces it, but God, who
creates natural friends in kinsmen. For every other thing in this world
man desireth either because it will help him to power, or to get some
pleasure, save only a true friend; him we love for love's sake and for our
trust in him, though we can hope for no other return from him.
Boethius

In friendship we do not make use of one another, because the friendship
is not for our own sake, but for the reciprocal relationship, the giving
and receiving, in which more is brought into being than would
otherwise exist. Our grand object should be to transform the relation
of acquaintanceship, in which other people are things, into that of
friendship, in which others exist in their own right; unless we make
progress in that we waste out lives. The object of friendship is not to
make life pleasurable but to provide the social environment in which life
can be lived. Callousness, indifference, and the closing of the heart are
not merely the fatal enemies of society, they are the individual death to
which Hobbes referred.
C. B. Purdom: *Life Over Again*

From quiet homes and first beginnings
Out to the discovered ends,
There's nothing worth the wear of winning,
But laughter and the love of friends.
Hilaire Belloc

Gambling

Gambling challenges that view of life which the Christian church exists to uphold and extend. Its glorification of mere chance is a denial of the divine order of nature.

William Temple

There is nothing in the world more precisely unchristian than gambling: for gambling means getting instead of giving – it means deliberately seeking happiness by getting instead of seeking happiness by giving. However small the stake, the act of gambling is a cessation for the time being of that life of love which is the very existence of the Christian.

William Temple

GENEROSITY

God loveth those who act generously.

Koran

Act generously and God will be with you.

St. Catherine of Sienna

Give all thou canst; high Heaven rejects the lore
Of nicely calculated less or more.

William Wordsworth: *Within King's College Chapel*

GLORY

If you ask me what is Glory? Well I can't tell you, but I know that it is a hundred times better than Grace. Glory is beauty, moral and spiritual beauty, beauty infinitely real, infinitely exalted, yet infinitely near and infinitely communicable.

Henry Drummond: *The Greatest Thing in the World*

GOD

...is to look back and to look forward and to live now in the light of the looking back and the light of the looking forward. Etc.

D.E. Jenkins: *Jesus and God* quoted by J Neville Ward,
Use of Praying

God is not unknown. He is unknowable. The mystery in which he shrouds himself is not like a blanket of fog which the fresh winds of new truth will one day disperse.

Reverend Dr. Colin Morris: *Words and The Word*

What is it to live for God? To live for God is to find the work he wants us to do in this world and to do it with all our might.

Ida Saidder: *Missy Doctor Vellore*

Mystery is the presence of God. Man cannot with truth locate that presence. God is not outside or beyond the world; he is not above or below; he is neither within nor without. He is an undefined presence, which imposes itself upon man's experience without uncovering the secret of divine being.

Charles Davis: *God's Grace in History* quoted by Reverend Dr. Colin Morris in *Words and The Word*

When we think of God as spirit we should think not of an infinite spiritual essence in repose but of an infinite spiritual essence in action.

A. M. Hunter: *Commentary on John* (Forsyth)

It is a common place of theology that God can't directly be described. He can be thought and talked about only be images and pictures which point to Him – some of them homely pictures like Our Father, some of them metaphysical causality.

H. A. Williams: *Some Day I'll Find You*

The idea of God is that than which nothing greater can be conceived.

Anselm

God…that which concerns man ultimately.

Paul Tillich: *Systematic Theology*

To predicate personality of God is nothing else than to declare personality as the absolute.

Ludwig Feuerbach: quoted by John Robinson in *Honest To God*

What you put your final trust in is your God. The answer which Martin Luther gave to the question what it means to have a God, or what is God, was that what you hang your heart on and confide in is your God.

J.H. Oldham: *Life is Commitment*

Charles de Foucauld...began to drop into churches as he passed them and spent some time repeating one short prayer: "My God, if you exist, make me know you".

Neville Ward: *Use of Praying*

He who does not have a God to thread his needle, does not have a God to give him salvation either.

Elsie Averduck: quoted by **Bishop Dibelius,** *In the Service of the Lord* (Autobiography)

We should not talk about God, only to Him.

Thomas Aquinas

Those who believe they believe in God, but without passion in their heart, without anguish of mind, without uncertainty, without doubt and even despair, believe only in the idea of God, not in God Himself.

URC Reports to Unamuno quoted Assembly 1976

GOD - KNOWING

But to find or know God in reality by any outward proofs, or by anything, but by God himself made manifest and self evident in you, will never be your case, either here or hereafter.

William Law: *Works, from Way to Divine Knowledge*

To know God is to learn how to make our lives eternal.

Dante

The path from the human to the divine goes through Calvary.

Abbé Henri Godin; quoted by Maisie Ward in *France Pagan? The Mission of ABBE Godin*

No one will ever be able to know the love of God and teach it to anyone else until he is reconciled with God and everyone else...so enter into your inner room and pray, pray, pray.

Apolo Kivebulaya: *Apostle to the Pygmies*

It is not hard to know God, provided one will not force oneself to define Him.

Joubert quoted by **Thomas Keir:** *The Word in Worship*

God does not die on the day when we cease to believe in a personal deity, but we die on the day when our lives cease to be illuminated by the steady radiance of wonder, the source of which is beyond all reason.

Dag Hammerskjold: *Markings*

I sought God for thirty years; I thought it was I who desired Him, but no, it was He who desired me.

Abu Yasid: quoted by F. C. Happold in *Mysticism*

Let him who would have an experience of God take up a task that is too great for him and then pray.

Dr. A Herbert Gray

GOD THE INDWELLING

I sought my soul, but my soul eluded me;
I sought my God, but my God eluded me;
I sought my brother - and found all three.

Unattributed

John Wesley passed at last into the presence of his Lord with the repeated words on his lips as he lay dying, "The best of all is that God is with us."

Attributed by **C. F. Andrew** *Christ in the Silence*

GOSPEL

We talk of the Gospel as Good News. But in fact it is bad news for
some because it strikes at the heart of human egotism and selfishness.
Jesus recognised this when he claimed not to bring peace but a sword.
Reverend Dr. Colin Morris: *The Word and The Words*

GRACE

Grace in us is just the impress of God's grace.
Andrew A. Bonar: *Heavenly Springs*

I have found great need of grace and had had an opportunity to practise
some of the hardest lessons in Christianity; to bear indignities without
animosity, to pray for such as despitefully used me, to love my enemies,
to overcome evil with good.
Oliver Heywood

The grace of God in the heart of man is a tender plant in a strange
unkindly soil.
Archbishop Leighton: quoted by Newton Flew,
Jesus and His Way

GRATITUDE

Keep your eyes open to your mercies. That part of piety is eternal, and
the man who forgets to be grateful has fallen asleep in life.
Robert Louis Stevenson

Most Papuan languages have no word for 'thank you' and in the middle
of a prayer (in the native tongue) one would hear the words 'thank you'
taken over from English to supply the deficiency.
Rev. E.H. Vines of Australia: article in *L.M.S. Chronicle* January 1954

Gratitude does not consist of loving a person who does us a service in
return. It consists of profiting by the service that has been done so that
we can act as well as possible towards the whole of human kind and not

only towards the individual to whom we are grateful.

Frederick Paulhan quoted in *Readers' Digest* December 1963

I, bundle of loosely tied complexes that I was, did not possess that grace (i.e. of receiving). I could lend money, but I could not borrow it; I sometimes went to great trouble to render a service to a friend, but if the reverse happened, I felt ashamed, guilty and broke into a lot of profuse thanks. For a long time I believed that those were the signs of an unselfish and noble character. Until one day Maria remarked across the kitchen table: "You have the vanity to give but you lack the generosity to take."

Arthur Koestler: *The Invisible Writing*

GREATNESS

He is truly great that hath great charity. He is truly great that is little in himself and makes no account of any height of honour.

Thomas A Kempis: *Imitation of Christ*, Chapter 1, 3

GROWTH

We never are, but are forever only becoming that which it is possible to be.

Unattributed

GROWING OLD

I am still at work, with my face to the future. The shadows of the evening lengthen ... but the morning is in my heart... the testimony I bear is this, the best of life is hidden further on, hidden from our eyes beyond the hills of time.

Sir William Mullock, Chief Justice of Canada,
oldest judge in the British Empire on his ninetieth birthday.

Already at this time, though he was not yet thirty-one, Byron was conscious of a physical decay far in advance of his years, and of a corresponding overwhelming lassitude. "At thirty," he wrote, "there is no more to look forward to … my hair is half grey, and the crows foot had been rather lavish of its indelible steps."

Iris Oriago, Marchesa of Val d'Orcia: in *The Listener*, June 24th 1948

At 32, Stevenson writes that he was just beginning to understand his art.

Unattributed

Towards the end of his life, William James, the philosopher, affirmed that his belief in immortality was stronger than ever, "because he was just getting fit to live".
He grew old without ever growing up.

Said of Edward Lear on TV **Monitor** programme 21st May 1961

Always feel a growing of the Lord that is universal and everlasting.

George Fox

For every man the trials of life grow deeper as character develops, though he may be spared the Job-like trials of Newton's old age; and with these deeper trials comes usually a compensating serenity.

Bernard Martin: *John Newton*

Yesterday and today I have had some glimpses within the veil, as if to prepare me more for what may now soon come. It is very solemn to find myself near the threshold of eternity, my ministry nearly done and my long life coming to its close. Never was Christ more precious to me than He is now.

Andrew A. Bonar: *Heavenly Springs* September 25th 1891

Corot, the painter, said in his seventy-seventh year; "If the Lord lets me live two years longer, I think I can paint something beautiful".

Unattributed

Life's evening ever brings with it its own lamp.

Joseph Joubert

On his 70th birthday Sir Alexander Fleming was asked what was the formula for a happy old age. He said: 'Keep on working'.

John Rowland: *The Penicillin Man*

HAPPINESS (OF A MOTHER)

Those who like me, have done many of the pleasant things they ought to have done, and their fair share, perhaps a littler more, of the equally pleasant things they ought not to have done, know that the happiness of having a family outdoes them all! The Dolomites are lovely reflected in the lake of Carezzo, and there was that one unbelievable night sky I saw when camping in Arctic Lapland; Kreisler answering Austrian encore with encore after encore was unforgettable, and there are other things... But I would exchange the lot if I had to choose, for the sight of two of my own children grubbily playing in a sandpit and the other three gaily setting off for a cycle ride. It matters little to me that I've had the good times, or that there are many other things that maybe I'll do someday, in comparison with the solid, lasting, vivid happiness of having my own children.

Alison Hawgood: *A Family is Fun*

And this is the happy life, to rejoice to thee, of thee, for thee, this is it, and there is no other.

St. Augustine: *Confessions*

Happiness is the inner concomitant of neat harmonies of body, spirit and society: and these harmonies are bound to be infrequent.

Reinhold Niebuhr: *The Irony of American History*

Happiness is the interest that is paid men by nature for investments in the good life. It is not the reward of perfection. It began as a dividend on the first step in the right direction and it accrues by compound interest.

Bevan Wolf: *How to be Happy Though Human*

Call no man happy till he dies: he is at best but fortunate.

Solon: *Herodotus c. 640-558 BC*

I am fulfilling in every case to the best of my ability the obligation of
being happy.

Joseph Joubert; attributed, Sidney Moore M.A.,
article in *Congregational Quarterly* July 1955

Man has not yet learned to enjoy himself: that is his greatest sin.

Friedrich Nietsche; quoted by Werner Pelz

The substructure contains the four main pagan virtues, taken from
Plato: courage, temperance, wisdom, and the all-embracing justice.
These produce natural happiness. Happiness does not mean having
a good time or having fun, but the fulfilment of one's own essential
nature.

Paul Tillich: *History of Christian Thought*

The more and more profoundly people love, the happier they are as
Christianity understands happiness.

J. Neville Ward: *The Uses of Praying*

HATE

Let no man pull you so low as to make you hate him.

Booker T. Washington; quoted by Martin Luther King

I resolved that I would permit no man to narrow and degrade my soul
by making me hate him.

Booker T. Washington; quoted by Harry Emerson Fosdick in
Twelve Tests of Character

Luther said: my soul is too glad and too great to be at heart the enemy
of any man.

Harry Emerson Fosdick: *The Manhood of the Master*

HEARING

Hearing in scientific terms is a varying number of vibrations on the eardrums. Intellectually it is composing those sounds into a comprehensible pattern of words: spiritually, it is expressing those ideas in appropriate behaviour.

The Reverend Maldwyn Edwards: *Daily Bible Studies* Sept. 10th 1957

HEAVEN

Heaven is not a faraway place to which we hope to go; it is the presence of God in which we ought to live.

W. R. Inge

What is heaven to a reasonable soul? Naught else but Jesus.

Martin Luther

Genuine immortality does not mean more existence; it means existence in contact with God.

T.H. Robinson: *Job and His Friends*

HEDONISM

It has always seemed to me that the only intelligent and satisfactory principle of life is that of determining both to have one's cake and eat it.

Ethel Mannin: *Confessions and Impressions*

When a New York socialite commented to Mrs. Fritz Kreisler that she didn't seem to get much of a kick out of social life, Mrs Kreisler answered, "No, I get more of a kick feeding poor children…I must get my kicks in a different way, that's all."

Quoted by Arthur Preston, "Greater Than Ourselves" in *Christianity Today*

HELL

Hell is not to love anymore. As long as we remain in this life we can still deceive ourselves, think that we live by our own will, that we love independently of God. But we are like madmen stretching out hands to clasp the moon reflected in water.

George Bernanos: *Diary of a Country Priest*

Hell is other people.

John Paul Sartre: *Huis Clos* (In Camera)

No person in Hell has the slightest pleasure in other people.

John Ciardi: Translation of Dante's *Inferno* and *Paradiso*

Hell, I maintain, is the suffering of being unable to love.

Dostoevski

Hell is not where the damned are, but what the damned are.

John Ciardi

Hell is the alternative to being grasped and held by a power that is stronger than death. Hell is eternal death.

David Edwards: *Last Things Now*

I thought, "Is any pain like this?" And I was answered in my reason – "Hell is another pain, to despair is there."

Julian of Norwich

Commenting on Lowry's novel 'Under the Volcano', Philip Toynbee says that, an enforced and perpetual threat to one's identity is the true nature of "being in hell". Hell is that negative separation from God and ones fellows that leads to inner despair and disintegration. Jesus Christ spent much of his time in his ministry freeing people from their hell on earth.

Rev. Noel Shepherd: *Prayer Fellowship Handbook* 1970

Hell is the eternal condition of those who have made relationship with God and their fellows an impossibility through lives which have destroyed love…Heaven, on the other hand is the eternal condition of those who have found real life in relationships through love with God and their fellows.

Richard Tatlock: in *In My Father's House*

HOPE

Dewdrops are the gems of morning
But the tears of mournful eve!
Where no hope is life's a warning
That only serves to make us grieve

Samuel Taylor Coleridge: *When we are old* from *Youth and Age*

Hope is a divinely infused quality of the soul, whereby with certain trust we expect those good things of life eternal, which are to be attained by the grace of God.

Thomas Aquinas

What oxygen is for the lungs, such is hope for the meaning of human life. Take oxygen away and death occurs through suffocation, take oxygen away and humanity is constricted through lack of breath; despair supervenes, spelling the paralyses of intellectual and spiritual powers by a feeling of the senselessness and purposelessness of existence. As the fate of the human organism is dependent on the supply of oxygen so the fate of humanity is dependent on the supply of hope.

Emil Brunner: opening words of *Eternal Hope*

If we are hopeful, in the Christian sense of the word, we shall live and think and work with the resolute conviction that the goal and aim of human life, for ourselves and for others, is that which the bible declares it to be … to be conformed to the Son of God, to be like him, seeing him as he is.

Bishop Frances Paget; quoted by Dean Inge in *Personal Religion and the Life of Devotion*

Hope is not impatient. It knows that God takes thousands of years to accomplish his purposes; but it is content to know that there is that going forward in the world with which a man may link his labour without spending it in vain.

Dean Inge

Hope is faith turned to the future, a vision inspired and sustained by love.

A.B.D. Alexander: *The Ethics of Saint Paul* quoted by Newton Flew in *Jesus and His Way*

Hope is an inward attitude of one who is committed to an enterprise. Fundamentally, it is an act of trust.

J.H. Oldham: *Life is Commitment*

You cannot imagine what an advantage we Christians have in prison over those who have no hope. Some of them are brave, but somehow still despairingly sad.

Ludwig Steil, Pastor in Prison: *Dying We Live*

When we sink at the grave, why the grave has scope,
And over the coffin men planted HOPE!
And it is not a dream of a fancy proud,
With a fool for its dull begetter;
There's a voice at the heart proclaims aloud –
"We are born for a something Better!"
And that voice of the heart, oh ye may believe,
Will never the hope of the soul deceive.

Friedrich Schiller: *Hope* translated by Lord Lytton

HEROISM

Heroism is the brilliant triumph of the soul over the flesh – that is, over fear; fear of poverty, of suffering, of calumny, of sickness, of isolation and of death. There is no serious piety without heroism. Heroism is the dazzling and glorious concentration of courage.

Henri Frederic Amiel: *Journal* 1st October 1849

Holy, Holiness

When we use the term 'holy' we must be sure that we mean by it no less than Isaiah – the Radiant Presence of Absolute Righteousness. Holiness must always be personal and moral – a call to worship and service in reverent affection.

E.V. Heaton: *His Servants the Prophets*

God will not use you for any special errand if you are not daily near Him. A bright spark comes out of the furnace. Ah, but the furnace was well heated before.
I am more than ever convinced that unholiness lies at the root of our little success. 'Holy men of God' spake to the fathers. It must be holy men still that speak with power.

Andrew A. Bonar: *Heavenly Springs*

In our era, the road to holiness necessarily passes through the world of action.

Dag Haamarskjold: Secretary-General of the United Nations, killed in a plane crash in the Congo 1961

Let the wise beware lest they bewilder the minds of the ignorant hungry for action: let them show by example how work is holy when the heart of the worker is fixed on the highest.

F.C. Happold: *Bhagavad Gita* quoted in *Mysticism*

But the Holy is not only that which is; the Holy is also that which out to be, that which demands justice above all.

Paul Tillich: *Theology and Culture*

Holy Spirit

… In Him
The Holy Ghost
Is a poor little bird
In a cage
Who never sings

And never opens his wings,
Yet never, never
Desires to be gone away.
Caryll Houselander; quoted in *Prayer Fellowship Handbook* 1974

Humility, Humble

Unfailing peace is with the humble. But in the heart of the proud is
envy and frequent indignation.
Thomas A Kempis: *Imitation of Christ* Book 1 Chapter VII

Surely an unteachable spirit is one of the most tragic things in life.
George Meredith

How great would that man be were he not so arrogant!
God loves nothing better than humility.
Two later Jewish proverbs - *IBRA Daily Bible Studies*
August 13 1957

Humility, that low sweet root
From which all heavenly virtues shoot.
Thomas Moore (Irish poet, satirist, composer, and musician)

"The sideline has become the main job. I no longer have the opportunity
of time for the supreme task which the Lord has entrusted to me…I
find it repugnant to live in the midst of all this splendour. How people
admire me and grovel to me! How I'd love to tell them how miserably
modest I feel and that in my job here I want nothing but to do my duty."
Edward Seckesson: *Mahler: His Life and Times*
(Gustav Mahler letter to J and N Bauer Lechner)

Humility before the flower at the timberline is the gate which gives
access to the path up the open fell.
Dag Hammarskjold: *Markings*

The only wisdom we can hope to acquire
Is the wisdom of humility: humility is endless.

T.S. Eliot: *Four Quartets*

HYMNS, HYMN SINGING

How did I weep in thy hymns and canticles, touched to the quick by the voices of thy sweetly attuned church! The voices floated into mine ears, and the truth distilled into my heart, whence my affectionate devotion overflowed, and tears ran down, and happy was I therein.

Not long had the church of Milan begun to use this kind of consolation and exhortation, the brethren zealously joining with harmony of voice and hearts...etc.

Augustine: *Confessions:* Book 9

David Livingstone writes…that he has been singing a hymn...the hymn that kept singing in his heart was:
   Jesus the very thought of Thee
   With sweetness fills the breast.
He says, "It pleases me so, it rings in my ears as I wander in the wild, wild wilderness. I like to think of the love of Christ. It always warms my heart.

Unattributed

It is now a fortnight since the 75th birthday. What a grand day that was! I can still hear the hymns we sang in the morning and evening, with all the voices and instruments. "Praise to the Lord, the Almighty, the King of Creation...shelters thee under his wing and so gently sustaineth." How true it is and may it ever remain so!

   Dietrich Bonhoeffer *to his parents in his first letter to them after his imprisonment: Letters from Prison*

In looking through Das Neue Lied during these days I am constantly reminded how it is to you principally that I owe my enjoyment of the Easter hymns. It is a year now since I actually heard a hymn. But the music of the inner ear can often surpass that which we hear physically, so long as we really concentrate. Isn't that remarkable? Indeed, there is something purer about it, and in a way music acquires a 'new body'. etc.

Dietrich Bonhoeffer: *Letters from Prison*

IDEAS

Nothing is so important as an idea whose time has come.

Victor Hugo

IMAGINATION

The simplest acts of the imagination always appear to be useless, until they are completed or fulfilled.

Charles Morgan: *The Voyage*

The imagination is what providence uses in order to get men into reality, into existence, to get them far enough out, or in, or down in existence. And when imagination has helped them as far out as they are meant to go – that is where reality, properly speaking, begins.

Kierkegaard: *Journal* 1854

IMITATION

Imitation based on love...If we really love a person we generally try wittingly or unwittingly to be as like the beloved as possible. We long to share their experiences and their thoughts, to read the same books, to adopt their attitudes towards life. We grow to appreciate their tastes or try to make them share ours. Children learn rapidly from teachers they admire, friends acquire habits of thought and speech from in schools to present worthy objects for the children to imitate. Stories of great men will often fire a child's imagination and make him try to resemble his hero. But it is well to select the heroes carefully, or at lease to select from their doings those which we really wish to have imitated, otherwise there is a danger that a false ideal may be formed.

Stuart and Oakden: *Modern Psychology and Education*

IMMORTALITY, LIFE ETERNAL

We should begin with the fact, if we are Christians at all (for it [i.e. the doctrine of immortality] just means our part and lot in the Christ who vanquished death) and we should act accordingly. I do not see how a true believer in Christ can doubt the immortality of those who are Christ's (and He claims all) or require occult assurance of it, which means finding Him unsatisfactory.

P. T. Forsyth: *This Life and The Next*

Towards the end of his life, William James, the philosopher, affirmed that his belief in immortality was stronger than ever because he was "just getting fit to live".

From *Congregational Prayer Fellowship Handbook* 1970

INCONSISTENCY

A constant dwelling on the sufferings of Christ and of the martyrs may produce in the emotional Christian an altogether admirable indifference to his own pains; but unless he is very careful to cultivate a compassion commensurate with his courage, he may end by becoming indifferent to the pains of others. The child who had sobbed so bitterly because they had hurt and killed poor Jesus was father of the man who fifty years later, did everything in his power to prolong a war which had already caused the death of hundreds of thousands of his fellow creatures and was reducing the survivors to cannibalism.

Aldous Huxley: *Grey Eminence*
(of Father Joseph of Paris (1577-1638))

INDECISION

The man who insists upon seeing with perfect clearness before he decides, never decides. Accept life and you must accept regret.

Henri Frederic Amiel: *Journal*

Influence

...The Benedictine order owed its existence to the apparent folly of a
young man who, instead of doing the proper sensible thing, which was
to go through the Roman schools and become an administrator under
the Gothic Emperors, went away and for three years lived alone in a
hole in the mountains. When he had become 'a man of much orison'
he emerged, founded monasteries and composed a rule to fit the needs
of a self perpetuating, hard-working contemplatives. In the succeeding
centuries, the order civilised North Western Europe, introduced or re-
established the best agricultural practice of the time, provided the only
educational facilities then available and preserved and disseminated the
treasures of ancient literature. For generations Benedictinism was the
antidote to barbarism. Europe owes an incalculable debt to the young
man who, because he was more interested in knowing God than in
getting on, or even 'doing good' in the world, left Rome for that burrow
in the hillside above Subiaco

Aldous Huxley: *Grey Eminence*

Their failure is a fountain
To which my mind for courage looks,
By instinct drawn to drink my fill,
As the hart desires the water brooks.

Richard Church: *Twentieth Century Psalter*

Nothing opens the eyes or enlarges the mind like meeting greatness.

Sir Richard Livingstone: *The Listener* 9 June 1949

And a calm even spirit goes through rough work far better than
a furious one. Although therefore God did use at the time of the
Reformation some sour, overbearing, passionate men, yet he did not use
them because they were such, but notwithstanding they were so; and
there is no doubt he would have used them much more had they been
of a humbler, milder spirit.

John Wesley: *Journal - No other Foundation*

Emmerson was himself a frail old man when his oldest friend
Longfellow died. They took him into the room where the body of his

friend was lying, and for a while Emerson stood looking at the dead poet's face. Then he was overheard to say, "He was a beautiful soul … but I have forgotten his name."

Alan Balding: *No Other Foundation*

INSPIRATION

One impulse from a vernal wood
Will teach you more of man,
Of moral evil and of good
Than all the sages can.

William Wordsworth: *The Tables Turned*

There is an immeasurable distance between the things which the imperfect imagine: and those which the illuminated behold through revelation from above.

Thomas A. Kempis: *The Imitation of Christ*

An idea becomes close to you only when you are aware of it in your soul, when in reading about it, it seems to you that it has already occurred to you, that you know it and are simply recalling it. That's how it was when I read the Gospels. In the Gospels I discovered a new world: I had not supposed there was such a depth of thought in them. Yet it all seemed so familiar; it seemed that I had known it all long ago, that I had only forgotten it.

Tolstoy: as recorded in *Mikhail Bulkagov's Diary* 18th April 1910.
(See Malcolm Muggeridge *Jesus*)

INTELLECT

Nothing influences our conduct less than do intellectual ideas.

Carl Jung: *Modern Man in Search of a Soul*

INTOLERANCE

Men often hate each other because they fear each other; they fear each other because they do not know each other; they do not know each other because they cannot communicate; they cannot communicate because they are separate.

Martin Luther King

INVOLVEMENT

I now began for the first time to envy those young cubs at the university who had fine scholars to teach them what was what. But now I pity undergraduates when I see what frivolous lives many of them lead in the midst of fleeting opportunity.
After all, a man's life must be nailed to a cross, either of thought or action.

Winston S. Churchill

JESUS - see Christ

JOY

Joy is the emotional experience which our kind father in heaven has attached to the discharge of the most fundamental of all the higher activities – namely those of inner growth and outer creativeness. Joy is the triumph of life; it is the sign that we are living our true life as spiritual beings.

Dean Inge: *Personal Life and the Life of Devotion*

Joy is the effective tone which accompanies the expression of any one instinct in conformity with the sentiments of self.

J. A. Hadfield: *Psychology and Morals*

Love is the motive for working: joy is the strength for working.

Andrew A. Bonar: *Heavenly Springs*

Joy is the signal that we are spiritually alive and active. Wherever joy is, creation has been; and the richer the creation, the deeper the joy.

W. R. Inge

The cutting edge of goodness is always joy and the radiant life.

B. C. Plowright: *Everyman Prays*

"When I heard Beethoven's Ninth Symphony," says Claudel, "I knew there was joy at the heart of the universe."

Leslie Weatherhead: *The Christian Agnostic*

Psychologically, joy is the index of health resulting from the adequate engagement of the affections and the vigorous and harmonious exercise of the powers. It is the sign that the soul has found its object.

Unattributed

JUDGEMENT – GOD'S

Jesus will always supply us with the best criticism of Christianity.

Unattributed

When the evening of this life comes you will be judged on love.

St John of the Cross

JUDGEMENT – OF OTHERS

I saw how people read the Scriptures without a right sense of them, and without duly applying them to their own states. For when they read that … least in the Kingdom of God is greater than John, they read these things and applied them to others.

George Fox: *Journal*

Turn thine eye upon thyself: and beware thou judgest not the actions of others. In judging of others a man labours in vain: often errs, and easily sins: but in judging and examining himself he always labours fruitfully.

Thomas A. Kempis: *Imitation of Christ*

The only wisdom I acquired when I travelled through Asia in search of Yoga and Zen masters was a lesson childishly simple once one had learnt it: never ask yourself whether a man is a saint or a phoney, but try to draw a balance sheet of the saintliness and phoneyness in him.

Arthur Koestler: in review of *Antimemoirs* by
André Malraux, *Sunday Observer* 22 Sept 1968

Everything has two handles, one by which it may be borne, the other by which it cannot. If your brother be unjust, do not take up the matter by that handle – the handle of his injustice – for that handle is the one by which it cannot be taken up: but rather by the handle that he is your brother and brought up with you; and you will be taking it up as it can be borne.

Epictetus

We will go before God to be judged and God will ask us, "Where are your wounds?"
And we will say, "We have no wounds."
And God will ask, "Was nothing worth fighting for?"

Dr. Allan Boesak

JUSTICE

It is by justice that we can authentically measure man's values or his nullity … the absence of justice is the absence of what makes him a man.

Plato

He who is less than just is less than man.

Anon

Justice may be defined as what Christian love does when confronted by two or more neighbours.

Paul Ramsey

KINGDOM OF GOD

The Kingdom of God in its full reality is not something which will happen after other things have happened. It is that to which men awake when this order of time and space no longer limits their vision.

C. H. Dodd

...What we find is power in complete subordination to love; and that is something like a definition of the kingdom of God.

William Temple: *Readings in St. John's Gospel*

KNOWLEDGE

Of the three ways of acquiring knowledge – authority, reasoning and experience, only the last is effective.

Roger Bacon: quoted by Leslie Weatherhead in *The Christian Agnostic*

LEADERSHIP

He broke fresh ground - because and only because, he had the courage to go ahead without asking whether others were following or even understood.

Dag Hammarskjold: *Markings*

LIBERTY

There are two kinds of liberty. The false, where a man is free to do what he likes, and the true, where a man is free to do as he ought.

Charles Kingsley

Liberty is born a twin; liberty and loyalty belong together.

Harry Emerson Fosdick

LIBERALISM

The strength of liberalism lies in its recognition of the need for Christianity to be applied to the human situation; its weakness lies in its readiness to discard or to ignore the brute historical scandal of Christianity in order the more readily to apply its tenets to society. For illiberal idealism and modernism lose touch with the completeness of the Word of God.

R. Gregor Smith: *The Free Man*

LIFE

The Gospel works not by revealing a law but by kindling a life.

Anon

What makes a man a Christian is neither his intellectual acceptance of certain ideas nor his conformity to a certain rule, but his possession of a certain spirit and his participation in a certain life.

Baron Fiedrich Von Hugel

A being breathing thoughtful breath,
A traveller between life and death;

William Wordsworth: *She was a Phantom of Delight*

It isn't enough merely to warm both hands at the fire of life – though not so very many people succeed in doing even that these days – the art of living lies in warming one's whole body and to be able to complete each new day with the thought that if one died on this day or the next, one would have had, as we say, a pretty good run for the money – and the pains.

Ethel Mannin: *Confessions and Impressions*

It is not growing like a tree
In bulk doth makes a man better be;
Or standing long an oak, three hundred year,
To fall at last, dry, bald and sere
A lily of a day

Is fairer far in May
Although it fall and die that night -
It was the plant and flower of light.
In small proportions we just beauties see;
And in small measures life may perfect be.

Ben Jonson

Perhaps the most revealing thing Chaplin has said and the most typical, was the reply he gave to Sam Goldwyn's question, "What do you want most from the future?" Chaplin was a young man then and he replied, "More life. Whether it comes through pictures or not – more life."

Cotes and Niklaus: *The Little Fellow*

They take life forward.

Walt Whitman's assessment of Scott and Cooper

You must suffer to be an artist. But not too much. To live is to suffer, and who tells children this is not so is dishonest – cruel.

Maria Callas

For life with all it yields of joy or woe is just our chance of the prize of learning love.

Robert Browning

Life is given us on the understanding that we defend it to the last.

Charles Dickens

Man was made for joy and woe
And when this we rightly know
Thro' the world we safely go.
Joy and woe are woven fine,
A clothing for the soul divine;
Under every grief and pine
Runs a joy with silken twine.

William Blake: *Auguries of Innocence*

In the morning when thou risest unwillingly let this thought be present
– I am rising to the work of a human being.

Marcus Aurelius

He looked like a soul, which has found a body by chance, and is trying
to make the best of it.
Said of Joseph Joubert by a friend
Life is a grindstone and whether it grinds a man down or polishes him
up depends on the stuff he is made of.

Joshua Billings

God likes life; He invented it!

Roger Fauré: friend of Paul Tournier

In the first place, life for the Christian is a dialogue with God. That
imparts to his life a steadiness and direction.

Dr. Oldham: *Life is Direction*

Be inspired with the belief that life is a great and noble calling, not a
mean and grovelling thing that we are called to shuffle through as we
can, but an elevated and lofty destiny.

William E. Gladstone: from *Morley's Life*, quoted by Edwards

We have become aware that in the great game which is being played we
are the players as well as the cards and the stakes.

Pierre Teilhard de Chardin: quoted by Greg. Smith in
The Free Man

No one can be asked a more important question than, "What is your
name?" If you can give a name in reply to that first question of the
catechism you have a very great possession, for to know your name is
to be aware of your own identity, to be able to differentiate yourself
from other people, and to feel that you possess your own life. Such an
experience as this means that you have a real measure of freedom.

E. N. Ducker: *Psychotherapy: A Christian Approach*

Bersenyev: It seems to me that to put oneself in second place is the whole significance of life.

Lewis: It seems to me that to discover what to put before oneself in the first place is the whole problem of life.

Charles Morgan: *The Fountain*

We need to stop asking about the meaning of life and instead think of ourselves as those who are questioned by life... He goes on to quote Nietsche, "He who has a 'why' to live for can bear almost any 'how'.

Viktor Frankl: Austrian psychiatrist, whose life included a spell in a Nazi death camp. Quoted by Reverend *Dr*. Colin Morris in *The Word and the Words*

The way to do is to be.

Lao Tzu: quoted Clare Rogers in *On being a Person* (Lao Tzu – twenty-five centuries ago)

To be that self one truly is.

Kierkegarde: *The Sickness unto Death*. Quoted by Clare Rogers in *On Being a Person*

LIGHT

She radiates light like a diamond, but not warmth.

Ethel Mannin: *Confessions and Impressions* (said of Rebecca West)

.

LITTLE THINGS

A little thing is a little thing, but faithfulness in a little thing is a big thing.

Japanese proverb

LOVE – GOD AND GOD'S LOVE

Faith founded the Church; hope sustained it. I cannot help thinking it is reserved for love to reform it.

Dean Stanley

Ultimate reality is incommensurate with our own illusoriness and imperfection; therefore it cannot be understood by means of intellectual operations; for intellectual operations depend on language and our vocabulary and syntax were evolved for the purpose of dealing precisely with that imperfection and illusoriness. Ultimate reality cannot be understood except intuitively, through an act of the will and the affections. 'Plus diligatur quam intelligatur' was a common place of scholastic philosophy. 'Love can go further than understanding'; for love enters where science remains out of doors. We love God in his essence but in his essence we do not see him.

Aldous Huxley: *Grey Eminence*

Whoso truly loves God must not desire God to love him in return.

Spinoza

For thus it was made out to me; I loved thee while thou wast committing this sin, I loved thee before, I love thee still, and I will love thee for ever.

John Bunyan: *Grace Abounding*

Let the love of Christ take possession of your heart, and you will find you are living for him without an effort.

Andrew A. Bonar: *Heavenly Springs*

He showed me a little thing the size of a hazel nut, lying in the palm of my hand; and it was as round as a ball. I looked thereupon with the eye of my understanding, and thought: what may this be? And it was answered generally thus: It is all that is made. I marvelled how it could last, for it seemed so little that it might suddenly have fallen to nought. And I was answered in my understanding; it lasteth and ever so small because God loveth it. And so the world hath its existence by the love of God.

Julian of Norwich

I never saw those heights and depths in grace and love and mercy as
I saw after this temptation – great sins to draw out great grace; and
where guilt is most terrible and fierce, there the mercy of God in Christ,
when showed to the soul, appears most high and mighty.

John Bunyan: *Grace Abounding*

What we most truly are in the depth of our soul refuses to surrender
to force – force from within no more than force from without. That is
what St. Augustine meant when he said that Christ's command to love
God is not obeyed if it is obeyed as a command. That is what St. Paul
meant when he said, "Though I bestow all my goods to feed the poor
and though I give my body to be burned and have not charity, it will
profit me nothing.

H. A. Williams: *The True Wilderness*

"Nobody ever touched me until you came," said a leper woman to a
missionary who was dressing her sores. "Now I know what love is."

From *LMS Ministers' Quarry* January 1952

Agape (love or charity) is energetic and beneficent good will which
stops at nothing to secure the good of the beloved object. It is
not principally an emotion or an affection; it is primarily an active
determination of the will. That is why it can be commanded as feeling
cannot.

C. H. Dodd: *Gospel and Law*

By love I do not mean any natural tenderness which is more or less in
people according to their constitutions; but I mean a larger principle of
the soul, founded in reason and piety which makes us tender, kind and
benevolent to all our fellow creatures, as creatures of God.

William Law: *Works*

Love found me in the wilderness, at cost
Of painful quests, when I myself had lost.
Love on its shoulders joyfully did lay
Me, weary with the greatness of my way
Love lit the lamp and swept the house all round,

Till the lost money in the end was found.
'Twas love, whose ever quick and watchful eye
The wanderer's first step homeward did espy
From its own wardrobe love gave word to bring
What things I needed shoes and robe and ring

R. S. Trench

Bertrand Russell, the agnostic, on his recent 80th birthday startled
many by a simple but great confession. "The root of the matter," he
declared, "is a very simple old fashioned thing, a thing so simple that
I am almost ashamed to mention it, for fear of the derisive smile with
which wise cynics will greet my words. The thing I mean – please
forgive me for mentioning it – is love – Christian love. If you feel you
have a motive for existence, a guide in action, a reason for courage, an
imperative necessity for intellectual honesty... Although you may not
find happiness you will never know the despair of those whose life is
aimless and void of purpose.

World Christian Digest January 1953

It is by love only that one keeps hold on reality.

Henri Frederic Amiel

Love at its highest point – love sublime, unique, invincible – leads us
straight to the brink of the great abyss, for it speaks to us directly of the
infinite and of eternity. It is eminently religious; it may even become a
religion etc.

Amiel's *Journal* 2nd September 1863

Love is the energy of a steadfast will bent on fellowship.

Walter Rauschenbusch

To turn all we possess into the channels of universal love becomes the
business of our lives.

John Woolman

Professor Herbert Butterfield, surveying as a historian, the influence
of Christianity on European history, says that Christianity 'is an ethic

which is dynamic and creative in that there is no telling what a man may do for love'.

Christianity in European History

Agape is that form of love in which God loves us and in which we are to love our neighbour – especially if we do not like him.

Paul Tillich: *Ultimate Concern*

Take heed to faith and hope; through these is begotten love towards God and man, love which gives eternal live.

Jesus; attributed by Macarius of Egypt in a homily, quoted by R. Newton Flew *in Jesus and His Way*

Let us believe, hope, love, someday there shall be victory.

St Augustine

Eric Fromm quotes a Franciscan father who said, 'the important thing is not whether people believe or don't believe but whether people care or don't care'.

BBC interview, *Listener* 27th October 1967

Now we have agreed that love is in love with what he lacks and does not possess.

Attributed to **Socrates** by Plato in *The Symposium*

Love consists in uncomprehending, grateful, wondering acceptance of love, ever undeserved, never to be earned" – love that is grace. For what is grace but simply loving for its own sake, without "getting anything out of it"?

Ida Gorres: *Broken Lights*

Love: the power of union – Dame Julian would say: oneing – and bearing fruit. Sex is the symbol which stands for it, not the thing itself.

Ida Gorres: *Broken Lights*

Love is the accurate estimation and supply of someone else's need.

C. F. Andrews

Love Thy Neighbour "I must make one confession," Ivan began. "I could never understand how one could love one's neighbours. It's just one's neighbours, to my mind, that one can't love, though one might love those at a distance…"

Fyodor Dostoyevski: Ivan in *Brothers Karamazov*

I'll love with you; I will not hate with you. I was not born for that.

Sophocles

Whoever loved that will not love for ever?

Euripides

Love has found many a hiding soul and brought it to light.

E. PhillPotts

Love is goodwill on fire.

B. C. Plowright: *Everyman Prays*

Love is the beginning and end of the law.

Judaism

The ways are two: love and want of love. That is all.

Confucianism

All beside love is but words.

Islam

To turn all we possess into the channels of universal love becomes the business of our lives.

John Woolman

Our two basic emotional reactions, our environment, self assertion and affection, are fused in the process of integration, to produce that combination of strength and sympathetic tenderness for which love is the true name. Love is more than tender feeling. It is strong capable of service and sacrifice for those for who we feel affection. In general human intercourse it is expressed as firm friendliness. In more intimate relationships it shows as determined persistence, purposefulness over long periods of time in considerate care for those who are the objects of our affections. In the life of the community it reveals itself as a capacity for genuine public spirit and disinterested endeavour for the welfare of the whole. This going out of oneself and giving of oneself to others is only possible in so far as we are not distracted and forced back upon the service of self by internal fears, conflicts and a sense of insecurity or stability in the personality itself.

H. Guntrip: *Psychology for Ministers and Social Workers*

One cannot even be just to one's neighbour, unless one loves him.

Sidney More: Article in *Congregational Monthly* July 1955

Love is the daughter of knowledge.

Leonardo da Vinci attributed to Ida Gorres

The 'new morality' is of course none other than the old morality, just as the new commandment is the old, yet ever fresh, commandment of love. It is what St Augustine dared to say with his 'dilige et quod vis fiac', which as Fletcher rightly insists, should be translated not 'love and do what you please' but 'love and then what you will, do.'

John Robinson

For God's sake hold your tongue and let me love.

John Donne

Love means loyalty rather than instinctive emotions. 'Treat your enemies as men' is the meaning, for any man has the right to kind treatment and sympathetic prayer.

Findlay: *Gospel According to St Luke*

For since the fall - listen carefully my son - to love is to crucify self for another.

Abbe Michael Quoist: *Prayers for Life*

Perfect love means to love the one through whom one became unhappy. But no man has the right to demand to be thus loved.

Soren Kierkegaard: *Journal*

Bruno Walter once said that 'Mahler loved humanity but forgot about man'.

E. Seckerson: *Mahler, His Life and Times*

Love without power is sentimental and anaemic: power without love is reckless and abusive.

Martin Luther King

This is all I have known for certain that God is love; even if I have been mistaken on this or that point, God is nevertheless love...He is love, not He was love, or he will be love, oh no, even that future was too slow for me, he is love.

Soren Kierkegaard: *Journal 1850*

He who knows nothing, loves nothing. He who can do nothing understands nothing. He who understands nothing is worthless. But he who understands also loves, notices, sees ... The more knowledge is inherent in a thing, the greater the love. ... Anyone who imagines that all fruits ripen at the same time as the strawberries know nothing about grapes.

Paracelcus quoted by Eric Fromm in *The Art of Loving*

MAN

I know my *Soule* hath power to know all things
Yet she is blinde and ignorant in all:
I know I'm one of Nature's little kings
Yet to the least and vilest things am thrall.

I know my life's a paine and but a span;
I know my *Sense* is mockt in every thing;
And to conclude, I know myself a MAN,
Which is a *proud* and yet a *wretched* thing.

Sir John Davies: *Nosce Teipsum*

What a piece of work is man? How noble in reason! How Infinite in faculty! In form and moving how express and admirable! In action how like an angel! In apprehension how like a God!

William Shakespeare: *Hamlet* Act 2 Scene 2

To become free and responsible. For this alone was man created and he who fails to take the way which could have been his shall be lost eternally.

Dag Hammarskjold: *Markings*

He (Teilhard de Chardin) quotes with approval Nietzsche's view that man is unfinished and must be surpassed or completed and proceeds to deduce the steps needed for his completion.

Julian Huxley: Introduction to Teilhard de Chardin's *The Phenomenon of Man*

The sin of each man... is not that he is a self but that being a self, he is self-centred.

William Temple

If this belief from heaven be sent
If such be Nature's holy plan
Have I not reason to lament
What man has made of man.

William Wordsworth: *Lines Written in Early Spring*

Man is only a reed, the feeblest reed in nature, but he is a thinking reed. There is no need for the entire universe to arm itself in order to annihilate him. A vapour, a drop of water suffices to kill him. Yet were the universe to crush him, man would still be more noble than that which slays him because he knows that he dies and the advantage the universe has over him; of this the universe knows nothing. Thus all our dignity lies in thought. By thought we must raise ourselves, not by space and time which we cannot fill. Let us strive then to think well - therein is the principle of morality.

Blaise Pascal: *Pensees*

A man worthy of his name is a man who can stand on his feet and face reality. He is the man who has allowed the Lord to transform his life at the deepest levels of his personality. "It's no longer I who live but Christ who liveth in me."

Michael Quoist: *Christian Response*

If we define man as that organism in which the dimension of spirit is dominant, we cannot fix a definite point at which he appeared on earth.

Paul Tillich: *Systematic Theology* Vol. III

MARRIAGE

When a man and woman love they dig a fountain to God.

Hindu proverb

MARTYRDOM (see Persecution)

... But there were some two hundred and seventy martyrs - little known men ... Everyone knows Latimer's bold words to his brother Bishop Ridley:'Be of good cheer, Master Ridley, and play the man, for we shall this day light such a candle in England as I trust by God's grace shall never be put out'. The candle was lighted doubtless. But it may be questioned if it was Latimer, Ridley, Cranmer and the greater martyrs who did most to light it. It is not easier for a bishop to be a martyr than for an ordinary poor man ... Ordinary men are more shocked by the suffering of the great, but more convinced by the heroism of their fellows ... There could be no doubt about Mary's Protestants, whose only guerdon was the martyr's death for conscience sake ...The determination which took simple folk to an agonising death by fire, rather than give up their faith, made the protestant cause.

W. Martin: *Groundwork of British History*

MATERIALISM

The world is too much with us, late and soon
Getting and spending we lay waste our powers:
Little we see in nature that is ours

We have given our hearts away, a sordid boon.

William Wordsworth: *The World is Too Much With Us*

MEDITATION

Meditation is a mental dwelling upon God which opens our nature to the divine inflow and maintains in devout Christians the life of God in the soul of man.

W. E. Sangster: *Teach us to Pray*

Meditation first; then follows the deed.

John Calvin

MEEKNESS

Meekness is but courage raised to its Nth degree, courage which reaches the point where it is willing to accept a blow - in body or in spirit - rather than wound.

B. C. Plowright: *Everyman Prays*

It takes us all our days to learn these two things - to be meek and to be lowly.

Andrew A. Bonar: *Living Springs*

MEMORY

Memory was given us that we might have roses in December.

J. M. Barrie

And I come to the broad fields and spaces of my memory, where are the treasures of innumerable images, brought into it from things of all sorts perceived by the senses ... When I enter there, I require what I will to be brought forth and something instantly comes; others must be longer sought for. These things do I within, in that vast court of my memory, for there are present within me, heaven and earth, sea and whatever I have perceived therein ... Great is this force of memory, exceedingly great, O my God, a large and boundless chamber! Whoever sounded the bottom thereof?

St. Augustine: *Confessions*

Albert Schweitzer was complimented on remembering so much. He replied, "Why should I lose my remembrances when I like them? When a human being becomes old he lives on his remembrances. All our discontents, ingratitude and self-seeking vanish away, and in a moment only our pleasant memories remain, hovering around us like spirits. First, I recall those quiet summer evenings in Friedrichsbrunn, then all the different parishes I have worked in, and then all our family occasions, weddings, christenings and confirmations - tomorrow my godchild will be confirmed. Innumerable memories come crowding in upon me, but only those which inspire peace, gratitude and confidence.

Dietrich Bonhoeffer: *Letter to his Parents from Prison*

He knew that he would be remembered, which is what most men want. As many people who have retired, he pottered around doing the unnecessary with extreme enthusiasm.

Dona Moraes: Mr. Ghandi said of Motifal Nehru.

MIRACLES

Miracles sometimes occur but one has to work terribly hard for them.

Charles Weizman

MISSION

A mission is the renewal of Christ's act in taking flesh and coming on earth to save us; a mission is the telling of the good news to men who do not know it. Both in its etymological sense and according to common speech the word "mission" signifies this sending forth of truth and light to men and societies that lack them

Maisie Ward: *France Pagan? The Mission of ABBE Godin*

Mission is often described as if it were the planned extension of an old building. But in fact it has usually been more like an unexpected explosion. By recording the growth of the church in mainly institutional terms we have suggested a slow even expansion and maturing, whereas the great leap forward and the sudden collapse have been such common features that we should have had the modesty to recognise that the breath of God has always played a more decisive part than our human strategy.

Bishop John V. Taylor: *The Go-between God*

MONEY

Money may be the husk of many things, but not the kernel. It brings
you food but not appetite; medicine but not health; acquaintance
but not friends; servants but not loyalty; days of joy, but not peace or
happiness.

Henrik Ibsen

MOTHERS

God could not be everywhere so he made mothers.

The Talmud quoted by H. E. Fosdick in *The Living of these Years*

NON-ATTACHMENT

The truth is that non attachment can be practised only in regard to
actions intrinsically good or ethically neutral. In spite of anything that
Krishna or anyone else may say bad actions are unannihilatable. They
are unannihilatable because, as a matter of brute psychological fact, they
enhance the separate personal ego of those who perform them. ... Any
act which enhances the separate personal ego, automatically diminished
the actor's chance of establishing contact with reality ...

Aldous Huxley: *Grey Eminence*

OBEDIENCE

Whoso would fully and feelingly understand the words of Christ must
endeavour to conform his whole life to Him.

Thomas A Kempis: *Imitation of Christ*

OPPORTUNITY

Each bud flowers but once and each flower has but its minute of
perfect beauty; so, in the garden of the soul each feeling has, as it were,

its flowering instant, its one and only moment of expansive grace and radiant kingship. Each star passes but once in the night through the meridian over our heads and shines there but an instant; so, in the heaven of the mind each though touches its zenith but once, and in that moment all its brilliancy and all its greatness culminate. Artist, poet or thinker - if you want to fix and immortalise your ideas or your feelings, seize them at this precise fleeting moment, for it is their highest point. Before it, you have but vague outlines or dim presentiments of them. After it, you will only have weakened reminiscences or powerless regret; that moment is the moment of your ideal.

Henri Frederic Amiel: *Journal* Dec. 30th 1850

There is a tide in the affairs of men,
Which, taken at the flood, leads on to fortune

William Shakespeare: Brutus, *Julius Caesar* Act IV Scene 3

OPTIMISM - SHALLOW

But though our religion appears too pure, too unselfish for mankind it is not really so, for we live in a noble, enlightened age...But now knowledge, freedom and prosperity are covering the earth; for three centuries past virtue has been steadily increasing, and mankind is prepared to receive a higher faith.

William Winwood Reade: *Martyrdom of Man*

OVERCOMING

There is no ill the body suffers, the soul may not profit by.

George Meredith

I never had in all my life so great an inlet into the Word of God as now. Those scriptures that I saw nothing in before were made in this place and state to shine upon me; Jesus Christ was also never more real and apparent than now; here have I seen and felt him indeed.

John Bunyan from prison (after twelve years): *Grace Abounding*

He said not that thou shalt not be tempested, thou shalt not be travailed, thou shalt not be distressed; but He said THOU SHALT NOT BE OVERCOME.

Juliana of Norwich (1342-1416)

Five storms tore their way down California that winter. We were caught out in three of them. This is the penalty of winter-sailing. But we learned more of our boat and of the sea in an our of storm struggle than in a summer of quiet sailing.

John Caldwell: *Family at Sea*

It is on defeats that victories are built.

Octavia Hill

How much virtue a man has is best seen on occasion of adversity. For occasions do not make a man frail; but they show what he is.

Thomas A Kempis *Imitation of Christ*

THE PARABLES

The Parables are weapons of war, aimed not like the Beatitudes at the inside circle of the Disciples, but at those outside - evangelistic weapons to bring them in.

Fison quoted in *IBRA Bibles Studies* 15-8-59

PATRIOTISM

O! My native country, that thou mightest be the first nation in this age of the world that might pass through the judgements of God, and be cleansed thereby and be happy.

Isaac Pennington

PERFECTION

No artist will ever surpass Phidias - for progress exists in the world but not in art. The greatest of sculptors will remain forever without an equal.

Rodin on Phidias, the Greek sculptor quoted by Fosdick

PERSECUTION

It belongs to my Christian profession to be vilified, slandered, reproached and reviled. And since all this is nothing else, as my God and my conscience do bear me witness, I rejoice in reproaches for Christ's sake.

John Bunyan: *Grace Abounding*

Made of unpurchaseable stuff
They went their ways when ways were rough
They, when the traitors had deceived,
Held the long purpose and believed:
They when the face of God grew dim
Held through the dark and trusted him
Brave souls that took the perilous trail
And felt the vision could not fail.

Edwin Markham: *The Shoes of Happiness*

PERSEVERANCE AND PATIENCE

I can plod, that is my only genius. I can persevere in any definite pursuit. To this I owe everything.

William Carey

We are sure to take the fortress if we can but persuade ourselves to sit down before it.

William Carey

The Christian Gospel is the revelation of God's patience, of the costliness of God's forgiveness. Such patience as we have shown has often been a sign of weakness; we have not cared enough to bother. But

God has always cared. He has cared enough not only to wait but to suffer.

Alan Balding: *No Other Foundation*

What does it matter if you arrive only after the hundredth attempt where another arrives at once? You will surely arrive if you do not allow yourself to be discouraged.

Confucius quoted by Paul Tournier in
The Strong and the Weak

POWER

Power is never good unless he who has it is good.

King Alfred the Great

PRAYER

Prayer is the grateful acceptance of the good which eternally belongs to us.

Dr. Stanley McKelvie

If we are right, and to be spiritually minded is to have the mind of Christ, then prayer is from first to last a school of courage, an exercise in manliness, and the spiritual life is a discipline in hardihood.

B.C. Plowright: *Everyman Prays*

Prayer is the activity by which we let God into our lives

Lewis Maclachlan: *Intelligent Prayer*

Prayer is not so much asking as receiving.

Lewis Maclachlan: *Intelligent Prayer*

Prayer is the act of thought by which we consent to God's will and admit it into our lives.

Lewis Maclachlan: *Intelligent Prayer*

Prayer is the simplest form of speech
That infant lips can try;
Prayer the sublimest strains that reach
The majesty on high

James Montgomery: *School Worship*

To pray means inevitably to challenge oneself in the light of Jesus Christ
and some at least do not pray because they unconsciously fear what they
would discover if that challenge were made.

B. C. Plowright: *Everyman Prays*

Then the Tempter again laid at me very sore, suggesting that neither the
mercy of God, nor yet the blood of Christ did at all concern me, nor
could they help me for my sin; therefore it was but in vain to pray. Yet
thought I, I will pray. But, said the Tempter, your sin is unpardonable.
Well, said I, I will pray, It is to no boot, said he. Yet, said I, I will pray.
So I went to prayer to God.

John Bunyan: *Grace Abounding*

In prayer we open ourselves up to the divine energy and grace
perpetually beating on us; and receive that energy and grace in order
that it may be transmuted by our living into work - may cleanse,
invigorate and slowly change us.

Evelyn Underhill: *Collected Papers*

The first thing that occurs to us is that all the machinery of prayer has
but one very simple object, our loving intercourse with God.

Evelyn Underhill: *Collected Papers*

If we allow ourselves to be unduly preoccupied with our own hearts, our
prayer life can degenerate into a pitiful narcissism. To keep the balance
true we must study Our Lord's perfect example here as elsewhere. For
Him, prayer was never allowed to become an emotional indulgence. It
was the girding of his loins for a journey, the trimming of his lamp for
the darkness, the putting on of his armour for the battle.

G. T. Jeffrey: *The Grace Wherein we Stand*

Prayer is seed sown on the heart of God.

Andrew A. Bonar: *Heavenly Springs*

After all, intercession is not asking God to do difficult things for Mr.
Jones or Mr. Smith (though. as you say, sometimes when we are deeply
concerned we can't help doing this). It is offering your will and love that
God may use them as channels whereby his spirit of mercy, healing,
power or light may reach them and achieve his purposes for them. We
can't do it unless we care, both for God's will and also for "the whole
family of man". But that certainly does not involve knowing all the
details about everyone who asks (for) our prayers. God knows the
details: we need not.

Letters of Evelyn Underhill

(Francis of Assisi) had been invited to spend a night in the house of a
rich citizen of Assisi. The two men slept in one room and soon after
they had retired to bed Francis rose silently and began to pray. Only
four words escaped his lips: "Deus meus et omnia". (My God and my
all) - but he continued to murmur these words over and over again till
daybreak.

J.H.R. Moorman: *St Francis of Assisi*

Pray inwardly, though thou think it suits thee not, for it is profitable,
though thou feel not, though thou see nought; yea, though thou
thinkest thou canst not. For in dryness and in barrenness, in sickness
and in feverishness, then is thy prayer well pleasing to me, though thou
think it suit thee nought but little. And so is all thy believing prayer
in my sight. God accepteth the goodwill and travail of his servant,
howsoever we feel.

P. Franklin Chambers: *Lady Juliana of Norwich*

Prayer is the only adequate confession of faith.

Wellhausen; quoted by J. S. Whale in
The Protestant Tradition

More things are wrought by prayer than this world dreams of.

Alfred Lord Tennyson: *King Arthur*

When asked, "What is the strongest argument for prayer?" He replied, "Sir, there is no argument for prayer."

Samuel Johnson

Work as though it all depended on you and pray as though it all depended on God.

William Carey

Prayer is openness to the ground of our being; and in it "the readiness is all."

John A.T. Robinson, Bishop of Woolwich:
Honest to God

Prayer is not conquering God's reluctance but taking hold of God's willingness.

Bishop Phillip Brooks

The Our Father contains all possible petitions; we cannot conceive of any prayer that is not contained in it. It is to prayer what it it to humanity. It is impossible to say it once through giving the fullest possible attention to each word, without a change, infinitesimal perhaps, but real, taking place in the soul.

Simone Weil

Prayer is our response to both the privilege and the responsibility whereby we cry Abba, Father! To engage in the mission of God, therefore, is to live this life of prayer, praying without ceasing, as St. Paul puts it, that is to say, sustaining a style of life that is focused upon God. This is indeed to engage in the mission of the Holy Spirit by being rather than by doing...etc.

Bishop John V. Taylor: *The Go-between God*

In the Christian view, prayer is principally the means which believers use to maintain their relationship with God, their responsiveness to his will for them, their particular understanding of life in terms of his revelation in Christ.

J. Neville Ward

Prayer is the ascent of the mind to God.

Lewis MacLacklan: *Intelligent Prayer*

Because charity is the power of God, the only power by which His kingdom can be extended amongst men, it will only be when we doubt the power of charity that we shall be troubled by the question, "Can our praying make a difference?" To pray is to open the heart to the entry of love - to ask God in; and where God is truly wanted, he will always come. By that union the universal working of the love of God has increase.

John Barnaby: "Soundings" quoted in the *Prayer Fellowship Handbook* 1970

Not for a lack of satisfying philosophy do our prayers run dry, but for Lack of love.

Harry Emerson Fosdick: *The Meaning of Prayer*

What we need is an understanding of prayer as withdrawal, rest, relaxation, preparation, even joy, recreation, 'a change', 'a holiday, a break. Prayer is exactly the renewal one man received from walking in his garden. etc.

John Vincent: *Here I Stand*

Words are only a means. However the silent prayer which has moved beyond words must always spring from everyday life, for everyday life is the raw material of prayer.

Abbe Michel Quoist: *Prayers of Life*

Prayer is the responsibility to meet God with all I have ... to expect to meet God in the way, not to turn aside from the way. All else is exercise towards that or reflection upon the depth of it.

Bishop John A. T. Robinson: *Honest to God*

Preaching

The first business of a clergyman awakened by God into a sensibility and love of the truths of the Gospel, and of making them equally felt and loved by others, is thankfully, joyfully and calmly to adhere to, and give way to, the increase of the new-risen light, and by true introversion of his heart to God, as the sole author of it, humbly to beg of Him that all he feels a desire of doing to those under His care may be first truly and fully done to himself.

William Law: *Character and Characteristics*

But while he (Arnold Bennett) with his keen observation of life, was telling people how to manage their lives he had no ideal for his own life worthy of his abilities.

Thomas Mee: *Staffordshire*

I have observed that a word cast in bye the bye hath done more execution in a sermon than all spoken besides. Sometimes when I thought I did no good, then did I most of all; and at other times, when I thought I should catch them, I have fished for nothing.

John Bunyan: *Grace Abounding*

Take heed to yourselves, lest you may unsay that with your lives which you say with your tongues, and be the greatest hinderers of the success of your own labours. It much hindereth our work when other men are, all the week long contradicting to poor people in private that which we have have been speaking to them from the word of God in public, because we cannot be at hand to manifest their folly: but it will much more hinder if we contradict ourselves and if your actions give the tongue the lie...One proud, surly, lordly word, one needless contention, one covetous action, may cut the throat of many a sermon.

Richard Baxter, to ministers of Worcester, quoted in *Philippians: Moffat's Commentary* (Dr. Moffat, Expositor)

I preached what I felt, what I smartingly did feel - even that under which my poor soul did groan and tremble to astonishment.

John Bunyan: *Grace Abounding*

I find more profit in sermons on either good temper or good works than in what are commonly called 'gospel sermons'. That term has now become a mere cant word; I wish none of our society would use it. It has no determinate meaning. Let but a pert, self-sufficient animal, that has neither grace nor sense, bawl out something about Christ or his blood or justification by faith and his hearers cry out, 'What a fine gospel sermon!'.

John Wesley: *Works* Edition 1872 Volume 13 P, 36
Quoted by Dr. Sangster: *Craft of Preaching*

People began discussing his sermons, and in letters to his friends he would often ask their prayers 'lest I become swollen headed' and would quote the story about St. Bernard, who when told by someone, 'Oh Father, your sermon was so excellent,' replied, shaking his head, Yes, I heard the devil say so when I had finished.'

Dom Bernard Clements

Have been struck at noticing how often, in going forth to preach, I was like one seeking his own entrance into the holy place and fellowship with God: not like one coming out from enjoying communion to speak to others.

Andrew A. Bonar: *Heavenly Springs* Feb 6th 1843

Mary Newton heard Wesley preach in London: Last night we heard Mr Wesley from John 5, 8, and 9. He spoke pretty enough from the former part of the chapter and he repeated several verses of different hymns. He spoke forty minutes, and there was nothing exceptional in what he said. There rather seemed to want something. When he had done preaching her spoke a considerable time about his illness in Ireland etc ... He spoke a long time and vastly well. I love to hear him, though I know him. He is clever and a very surprising man of his years.

Bernard Martin: *John Newton*

I wish to pray from this date every Sabbath morning before going out to preach, and every time I go to preach to stand still a little and praise the Lord for sending to sinners his glorious gospel.

Andrew A. Bonar: *Heavenly Springs* October 1, 1843

I find that whatever sorrow or humiliation of spirit passes on us, that should give way in some measure to a fresh taste of God's love when going forth to preach.

Andrew A. Bonar: *Heavenly Springs*

Did you ever feel in preaching as if you were a blunt arrow? I felt so yesterday until about evening, when the archer seemed to sharpen the point.

Andrew A. Bonar: *Heavenly Springs*

I preached in Wednesbury at four, to a nobler people, and was greatly comforted among them; so I was likewise in the morning, Wednesday 25th. How does a praying congregation strengthen a preacher!

John Wesley: *Journal* October 24th 1749

Dr. Black to Preachers: Your business is serious gunfire with a target. Heard a sermon about duty of all to give good example etc. but I fear he himself was guilty of not doing.

Samuel Pepys: *Diary* January 19th 1661

I was sent to feed the sheep, not to amuse the goats.

C. H. Spurgeon

"... But after three or four years Satan raised up some potent adversaries against him, who maligned and opposed him for the faithfulness of his plain admonitions. Some meetings took place about his continuance, one said to him, 'Mr. Heywood, you have raised differences and disturbances since you came'. He answered, 'I have not sought the peace of the place, but the good of it.'

Oliver Heywood: *Works* Volume 1
(said of Nathaniel Heywood, Minister of Illingworth Chapel).

Nor was he scant and short in his sermons, but usually long, two hours at least, often three, yea, sometimes he would even continue four or five hours, praying and preaching; his heart was so set on his master's work, that he forgot his own strength and his hearers' patience. Nor did he tediously dream over his work, but was full of zeal, vigour, tenderness and affection, often strained his voice beyond what his natural strength could well bear, which occasioned torturing and mortal disease. Like a candle he spent himself to give others light.

> **Oliver Heywood:** *Works* Volume 1
> (said of Nathaniel Heywood)

Observe it, they are ordinarily the soundest Christians that are trained under the most plain and piercing preaching: therefore I entreat you to lay yourselves directly under the manner of the word, to be framed by the Lord according to his will.

> **Oliver Heywood:** *Heart Treasure*

If a man is going to sleep in my congregation, don't wake him up, wake me up.

> **C. H. Spurgeon**

When you are called on to declare God's wrath, conceal your own.

> **Oliver Heywood:** *Soliloquies*

9th November 1851. At the church of St. Gervaise, a second sermon from Adolphe Monod. Subject: Paul or the active life of the Christian. I felt the golden spell of eloquence; I found myself hanging on the lips of the orator, fascinated by his boldness, his grace, his energy and his art, his sincerity and his talent; and it was born in upon me that for some men difficulties are a source of inspiration, so that what would make others stumble is for them the occasion of their highest triumphs. He made St. Paul cry during an hour and a half; he made an old nurse of him, he hunted up his old cloak, his prescriptions of water and wine for Timothy, the canvas that he mended, his friend Tychieus, - in short all that could raise a smile; and from it he drew the most unfailing pathos, the most austere and penetrating lessons. He made the whole of St. Paul, martyr, apostle and man, - his grief, his charities, his tenderness - live again before us, and this with a grandeur and unction a warmth of reality such as I had never seen equalled...Finally, as a peroration, he dwelt on the necessity for a new people, for a stronger generation if the world is to be saved from the terrors which threaten it. 'People of God, awake! Sow in tears that ye may reap in triumph!' What a study is such

a sermon! I felt all the extraordinary literary skill of it, while my eyes
were still dim with tears. Diction, composition, similes - all instructive
and precious to remember. I was astonished, shaken, taken hold of.

Henri Frederic Amiel: *Journal*

Many sermons are lost for want of people taking them home to their
closets, and turning them into prayer.

Oliver Heywood: *Works*

Neither was he voxet praeterim nihil, a mere voice and no more, as some
preachers who like thunder make a loud noise, without any distinct
or significant sound: no, his sermons abounded with solid divinity,
scripture arguments, alluring similes and heart-melting passages. He
was an excellent text man producing judicious(?) interpretations;
an experienced casuist, resolving cases of conscience with correct
discrimination. A clear disputant, stating controversies accurately and
distinctly, answering objections skilfully and satisfactorily and proving
the truth to a demonstration. He was a pathetic preacher, riveting the
nail by faithful appeals to the consciences of his hearers.

Oliver Heywood: *Works* Volume 1

(Of Nathaniel Heywood) Kerygma (translated 'preaching' in N.T.)
properly means a public announcement or declaration, whether by a
town crier, or by an auctioneer commending his goods to the public, or
by the herald of a sovereign state despatched on a solemn mission to
present an ultimatum, it may be, or to announce terms of peace.

C.H.Dodd: *Gospel and Law*

To be close to God is the only way of bringing God close to man.

Abbe Godin (see *France Pagan?* Maisie Ward)

Samson's strength was only indicated by his long hair. It had a secret
spring. Our success would not be our strength, nor would our enlarged
preaching and diligent visiting, yet these will begin to grow if we have
access to the hidden source.

Andrew A. Bonar: *Heavenly Springs*

O what a thing it is to have a curum animarum! You and I are called to this: to save souls from death; to watch over as those that must give account! If our office implied no more than preaching a few times in a week, I could play with it; so might God.

John Wesley: *Letter* 25th March 1772

Preaching, in Bernard Manning's phrase, was a manifestation of the Incarnate Word, from the written Word by the spoken Word.

W. E. Sangster: *The Craft of the Sermon*

I preached as never sure to preach again, and as a dying man to dying men.

Richard Baxter: *Love, Breathing and Thanks and Praise*

Bishop Quayle, the pulpit totem man of America's mid-west commented that preaching is not the art of making a sermon and then delivering it but of making a preacher and delivering that.

Quoted by **The Reverend Dr. Colin Morris:** *The Word and the Words*

Let those who feel themselves called upon to be prophets preach penitential sermons; We simple servants of God should preach in such a way that those who listen to us may always feel we are the saviours joyful people.

Bishop Otto Dibelius: *In the Service of the Lord*

Let no preacher give up the faith that God wants to do a deed through him.

Martin Luther quoted in *The Word and the Words*,
by the Reverend Dr. Colin Morris

Although I am old, experienced in speaking, I tremble whenever I ascend the pulpit.

Martin Luther quoted in *The Word and the Words*,
by the Reverend Dr. Colin Morris

Pride

But, I say, my neighbours were amazed at this my great conversion from prodigious profaneness to something like a moral life and sober man. Now, therefore, they began to praise, to commend, and to speak well of me, both to my face and behind my back. Now I was, as they said, become Godly: now I was become a right honest man. But oh, when I understood those were their words and opinions of me, it pleased me mighty well! For though as yet I was nothing but a poor painted hypocrite, yet I loved to talked of as one who was truly Godly. I was proud of my Godliness, and indeed, I did all I could either to be seen or well spoken of by men. And thus I continued for about a twelve month or more.

...But all this while, when I thought I kept this or that commandment, or did by word or deed, anything I thought was good, I had great peace in my conscience, and would think with myself, God cannot choose but be well pleased with me: yea, to relate it in my own way, I thought no man in England could please God better than I.

John Bunyan: *Grace Abounding*

Proof - of God

Let us remember that to this day true religion is as independent of facts as it was with the prophets. True religion is a conviction of the character of God and a resting upon that alone for salvation. We need nothing more to begin with; and everything else in our experience and fortune helps us only in so far as it makes that primary conviction more sure and certain...etc.

G. A. Smith: *Book of Isaiah*

Providence

There is a power whose care
Teaches thy way along that pathless coast,
The desert and illimitable air
Lone wandering, but not lost.
He who from zone to zone

Guides through the boundless sky
Thy certain flight
In the long way that I must
tread alone
Will lead my steps aright

William Cullen Bryant: *To a Water Fowl*

God's providence is the consistent pressure he has established in all life towards the total good of all human beings, towards the ultimate welfare of our whole beings (our bodies and spirits), towards the full development of our potential, towards the redemption of all creation. In all circumstances that pressure of love and fulfilment which is the power of God unto salvation is at work ceaselessly and indefatigably just as the north pole is ceaselessly attracting all compass needles to itself by virtue of the magnetism built into the structuring of the whole world. That is how God works.

Jones and Wesson: *Towards a Radical Church*

PURGATORY

Perhaps it is God's plan that we should wait for purgatory before we begin to be confronted with a great deal of what is inside us etc ... or to put into religious language, when we receive more of what we are it means that for us purgatory has begun.

H. A. Williams: *The True Wilderness*

PURE IN HEART (SINGLE-MINDEDNESS)

Let nothing be great unto thee, nothing high, nothing pleasing, nothing acceptable; but simply God or that which is of God.

Thomas A Kempis: *Imitation of Christ*

If thou seekest Jesus in all things, thou shalt surely find Jesus. But if thou seekest thyself thou shalt also find thyself.

Thomas A Kempis: *Imitation of Christ*

QUIETNESS

The dew does not fall on a windy night; it is when all is still.

Andrew A. Bonar: *Heavenly Springs*

To acquire heart treasure withdraw from the world. At some times learn to sequester yourselves from the cares, affairs. comforts, cumbers and company here below. Do not think you can hoard up in a crowd. Satan loves to fish in troubled waters. But so doth not Christ... in this you must be separatists.

O. Heywood: *Heart Treasure.* He concludes by quoting Herbert's "By all means use some time to be alone". etc.

I believe in the discipline of silence and could talk for hours about it.

George Bernard Shaw

Silence is the element in which great things fashion themselves.

Thomas Carlyle

It was said of Carlyle, "He preached the gospel of silence in twenty volumes."

William Barclay: *Gospel of Mark*

The Indian religions train men to recollectedness... we are too much inclined to imagine that Christianity is merely activity. We do not have enough inwardness, we are not sufficiently preoccupied with our own spiritual life, we lack quietness.

Albert Schweitzer: *IBRA* 19 August 1970

Be silent about great things: let them grow inside you. Never discuss them; discussion is limiting and distracting. It makes things grow smaller. Before all greatness be silent. In art, in music, in religion be silent.

Baron Friedrich Von Huegel

Rationalisation

Some indeed have urged the holy kiss; but then I have asked them why they make their balks; why they did salute the most handsome and let the ill-favoured ones go.

John Bunyan: *The Pilgrim's Progress*

Reaction -
After Spiritual Experience

I have wondered much at this thing, that though God doth visit my soul with never so blessed a discovery of himself, yet I have found again that such hours have attended me afterwards that I have been in my spirits so filled with darkness that I could not so much as once conceive what that God and that comfort was with which I hade been refreshed.

John Bunyan: *Grace Abounding*

Repentance

The rejection of the negative with the whole of ones being is called repentance.

Paul Tillich: *Systematic Theology* Volume 3

Responsibility

The one thing God cannot relieve us of is our responsibility. Without it we might be the clay and he the potter, but we should not be children and he our father.

John Oman

Religion

Schliermacher defined religion as "the feeling of absolute dependence".

Paul Tillich: *Systematic Theology*

Whitehead defined religion as "the attitude which the individual takes up towards the determiner of his destiny".

Professor J. Bisset Pratt

"What we do with our solitariness".

A. N. Whitehead

"The feelings, acts, and experiences of individual men in their solitude, so far as they apprehend themselves to stand in relation to whatever they may consider the divine."

William James

"The experience of human nature in the higher ranges of its activity".

J Haynes Holmes

"The definition of religion as self-transcendence of life in the dimension of the spirit."

Paul Tillich

Religion is not a form of experience existing separately from other forms of experience. It is the transfiguration of the whole of experience. The constant temptation of the church is to lose sight of this truth, and consequently to compress the fullness of living reality into hard and fixed intellectual formulations and rigid moral codes and forms of activity which are too narrow to hold the rich exuberance of life.

Unattributed

"a felt practical relationship with what is believed in as a superhuman being or beings."

R.H. Thouless: *The Psychology of Religion*, quoted by Guntrip in *Mental Pain and the Cure of Souls*

"I would prefer to describe religion as experiencing a relationship with the ultimate all embracing reality regarded as personal."

H. Guntrip: *Mental Pain and the Cure of Souls*

Religion is knowing profoundly what you know already.

Blaise Pascal

Religion is the self-transcendance of life in the realm of the spirit.
Harry Guntrip: *Mental Pain and the Cure of Souls*

Religion is response to God. True religion will be the right response to God in that environment in which our lives are set.
Nathaniel Micklem: *A Religion for Agnostics*

Professor Whitehead is a very wise man but he once said a very silly thing: "religion is what a man does with his solitude"..
W. H. Auden in the foreword to
Dag Hammarskjold's *Markings*

The greatest aim of all religion is to transfer the centre of interest from self to God.
William Temple: *Drew Lecture on Immortality*

RESIGNATION

...He lays emphasis on what he calls "Acts of Resignation". By this he means facing actual difficulties in our lives, things which are very likely to happen, or which are now happening and making acts of entire acceptance of the divine will in their regard. This exercise as he calls it is most salutary. When we reflect upon all the misery and turmoil and controversy about trifles that is caused by resistance to holy life as it comes to us, when we think of all the unhappy, disappointed, frustrated people we know, we realise how this spirit of acceptance would completely alter their lives.
Olive Wyon: *School of Prayer*

RESURRECTION

They have often been hammering the nails into the Church's coffin when she rose again.
Dr. George McLeod

REWARD

Every night my prayers I say
And get my dinner every day;
And every day that I've been good,
I get an orange after food.

The child that is not clean and neat
With lots of toys and things to eat,
He is a naughty child I'm sure -
Or else his dear papa is poor.

Robert Louis Stephenson: *A Child's Garden of Verses*

Just think of Eugene Sue, who has written himself into a millionaire
by describing poverty and misery: yes, he was capable of giving Rd50
to the poor for having been the fortunate man to whom the envious
opportunity was given - of playing the hero, the witness to the truth,
with applause and laurel leaves.

Soren Kierkegaard: *Journal* 1850

REVENGE

Certainly in taking revenge, a man is but even with his enemy: but in
passing it over, he is superior, for it is a prince's part to pardon... A man
that studieth revenge keeps his own wounds green which otherwise
would heal and do well.

Francis Bacon from *Essay on Revenge*

...Revenge, at first though sweet
Bitter ere long , back on itself recoils

John Milton: *Paradise Lost*

SACRIFICE - SELF

I have measured out my life with coffee spoons.

T. S. Eliot

Christ needs men who will think nothing of a few hardships and spurn the notion that the work here involves any sacrifice. I think the word "sacrifices" ought never to be used in Christ's service.

James Chalmers

The vine from every living limb bleeds wine:
Is it the poorer for that spirit shed? ...
Measure thy life by loss instead of gain,
Not by the wine drunk, but the wine poured forth
For love's strength standeth in love's sacrifice,
And whoso suffers most hath most to give.

Mrs. Hamilton King *The Disciples* quoted by C. F. Andrews:
Christ in the Silence

A sacrifice is any and every action in which we are brought to union with God in holy fellowship.

St. Augustine

If people ever speak to you of the things a missionary has to give up, tell them, from one who knows, that for every single thing one gives up, one receives back in happiness, friendship, in the joy of creative work, and I think, in a growing awareness of the Lord, much more than a hundredfold.

Constance Fairhall: *Island of Happiness*

I now began for the first time to envy those young cubs at the university who had fine scholars to tell them what was what ... But now I pity undergraduates, when I see what frivolous lives many of them lead in the midst of fleeting opportunity. After all, a man's life must be nailed to a cross either of thought or action. Without work there is no play.

Winston S. Churchill: *My Early Life*

Self Sacrifice may be worthless if there is no self worthy of being sacrificed. The other one or the other cause may receive nothing from it, nor does he who makes the sacrifice achieve moral self-integration from it.

Paul Tillich: *Systematic Theology*

SAINTS

A definition: "Because they were cheerful when it was difficult to be cheerful, and patient when it was difficult to be patient and because they pushed on when they wanted to stand still, and kept silent when they wanted to talk and were agreeable when they wanted to be disagreeable.

Unattributed

A believer is not very holy if he is not very kind.

Andrew A. Bonar: Heavenly Springs

I think it is a very poor kind of holiness that does not make us care for others.

Ibid

Saints are men and women who, amidst the whirr of the spindle in the mill and the clink of the scales on the counter and the hubbub of the market place and the jangle of the courts, are yet living lives of conscientious devotion to God.

Alexander Maclaren

Saints are those, who in life, in spirit and in deed, clearly and unmistakably show us that God lives.

Archbishop Soderblom

The state of saintliness is the state of transparency towards the divine ground of being: it is the state of being determined by faith and love.

Paul Tillich: Systematic Theology Volume 3

Saints are people who let the light through.

Unattributed

SALVATION

Salvation is a birth of life, but reason can no more bring forth this birth than it can kindle life in a plant or animal. You might as well write the word 'flame' upon the outside of a flint, and then expect that its imprisoned fire should be kindled by it, as to imagine that any images or ideal speculations of reason painted in your brain should raise your soul out of its state of death and kindle divine life in it.

William Law: *New Birth* in *Works*

Though psychological salvation consists in crossing over from one camp to the other, (i.e. from the weak to the strong) religious salvation lies in the rediscovery of the divine purpose, in which the instinct of life and the moral conscience each have the proper function in the person for which they were designed by God. No doubt that purpose is never fully realised in this world. But case after case has shown that the road to health both for the person and for society lies in a genuine experience of the grace of God.

Paul Tournier: *The Strong and the Weak*

And now we are saved absolutely, we need not say from what, we are at home in the universe, and, in principle and in the main, feeble and timid creatures as we are, there is nothing within the world or without it that can make us afraid.

Bernard Bosanquet on Salvation, quoted in *Mysticism*: F. C. Harold from *Test of Friendship*

SCIENTIFIC OUTLOOK ETC.

Nothing exists except matter and energy; man is a hairless monkey; therefore everyone must lay down his life for his friends.

Vladimir Solovyov 19th century philosopher, from a talk by S. Francis in *The Listener* 28th April 1949

I had rather believe all the fables in the Legend and the Talmud and the Alcoran, than that this universal frame is without a mind.

Francis Bacon: *Of Atheism*

Seeking to be a seeker is to be of the best sect next to a finder and such shall be every faithful, humble seeker at the end.

Oliver Cromwell

SELF-CONTROL

I think I see it as somewhat glorifying to God to keep our temper and happy frame of soul in the midst of common care or in the midst of a rush of earthly vexations or annoyances, as it would be under the blast of persecution and dread of sword and death. All the more glorifying too, in the sight of God, because none else may be witness, and no motive of vainglory can creep in.

Andrew A. Bonar: *Heavenly Springs*

And this should be our business to conquer ourselves: and daily wax stronger than ourselves: and make some growth in holiness.

Thomas A Kempis: *Imitation of Christ*

When you are called on to declare God's wrath, conceal your own.

Oliver Heywood

SELF-KNOWLEDGE

...But Thou, O Lord, whilst he was speaking, didst turn me round towards myself, taking me from behind my back where I had placed me, unwilling to observe myself, and setting me before my face, that I might see how foul I was, how crooked and defiled, bespotted and ulcerous. And I beheld and stood and aghast and whither to flee from myself I found not. And if I sought to turn mine eye from off myself, he went on with his relation, and Thou again didst set me over against myself and thrustedst me before my eyes, that I might find out my iniquity and hate it. I had known it but made as though I saw it not, winked at it, and forgot it.

St. Augustine: *Confessions* Book 8 para VII

An humble knowledge of thyself is a surer way to God than a deep search after learning.

Thomas A Kempis: *Imitation of Christ*

It is as hard to see oneself as to look backwards without turning round.
Henry Thoreau quoted by W. H. Auden in Foreword to Dag
Hammarskjold's *Markings*

SELF-RESPECT

Fine clothes are a great assistance to our good opinion of ourselves.
There is a story of a Frenchwoman who remarked that a well-fitting
frock gave a sensation of peace and well-being that religion was
powerless to convey.
Stuart Oakden: *Modern Psychology and Education*

To bring about a reformation in character it is necessary to re-establish
a person's self-respect. This fact is now widely recognised, and is part
of the policy of those engaged in prison reform. A man with no self
respect offers no handle to to the reformer, he has no sense of shame,
and is no more abashed than Falstaff when his faults are pointed out.
Stuart Oakden: *Modern Psychology and Education*

A child who is taught to believe that he is essentially good, though
subject to lapses which effort may cure, has a better chance of really
becoming good than one who is always being told that "he is a naughty
boy and likely to come to a bad end". In school, therefore, we must
refrain from labelling A as a dunce and B as untidy or C as a nuisance.
They quickly adopt this view of themselves and live up to it.
Stuart Oakden: *Modern Psychology and Education*

SERMON

From the first I realised that everything depended upon the sermon ...
those who came, came exclusively for the sermon.
Bishop Dibelius: *Autobiography*

I felt too inadequate to be able to hand on to the congregation with
authority, the word of the holy God - for that is what preaching really is.

This sense I have retained right up to my old age.

Bishop Dibelius: *Autobiography*

I had to preach with body, mind and soul as the Apostle Paul says in intimate contact with the congregation, and had to demand something from my congregation. My principle regarding a sermon has always been quite simple and straight forward. When the wife comes home and the husband asks her (or it may be the other way round, as the case may be) what did he say? She should be able to say quite definitely, he said this.

Bishop Dibelius: *Autobiography*

SERVING CHRIST/GOD

Christ has no body now on earth but yours, no hands but yours, no feet but yours; yours are the eyes through which is to look on Christ's compassion in the world, yours are the feet with which he is to go about doing good and yours are the hands with which he is to bless us now.

St. Theresa of Avila

Recall the twenty-one years; give me back all its experience, give me its shipwrecks, give me its standing in the face of death ... give it me back again with spears flying about me, with the club knocking me to the ground; give it me back and I will still be your missionary.

James Chalmers

God takes much pleasure in adverbs: it pleaseth not God that a duty be done except it be well done.

Oliver Heywood: *Works* Vol. III

My task is to build bridges, even when I can see the floods which will carry them away bearing down on them.

African pastor quoted in
Prayer Fellowship Handbook 1971

SIMPLICITY

Make my life simple and straight like a flute or reed for thee to play on.
Rabindranath Tagore

Beware of the terrible, light-hearted simplifiers. They create the most hopeless confusion in the long run.
Theodor Haecker: *Journal of the Night* quoted by Oldham in *Life is Commitment*

A wise man can hold his own here only if he can combine simplicity with wisdom ... because the simple man knows God.
Dietrich Bonhoeffer. Quoted by Mary Bosanquet, *The Life and Death of Dietrich Bonhoeffer*

SIN

Sin is that which impedes spiritual progress.
D. Kirk quoted by Martin Thornton in *The Rock and the River*

I don't use the word sin much - it is more a sense of waste.
Cyril Connolly, critic and man of letters

The sin of each man is not that he is a self but that being a self he is self-centred.
William Temple from "Come Alive", *Prayer Fellowship handbook* 1974

Whatever hurts another, demeans another, whatever make persons objects to be used, that is sin, the denial of God.
Congregational, *Prayer Fellowship Handbook* 1972

The greatest sin in the world is that of not caring.
Bishop Trevor Huddleston, attributed.

Sin means the power that separates us from God.
Paul Tillich: *Ultimate Concern*

Sin is essentially departure from God in thought and desire. It is
rebellion against God's will. And against the blessedness God has
appointed for us.

Lewis Machlachlan: *Intelligent Prayer*

Paul is trying to grapple with that rift in* personality given to the power
behind the unbelief which prevents us from thinking straight, which
led him to believe in Christ as an indication between the hidden God...
(**torn, covered in old brown opaque sellotape - illegible*)

Unattributed

Sin corrupts the highest as well as the lowest achievements of human
life. Human pride is greatest when it is based upon solid human
achievements.

Rheinhold Niebuhr

SLEEP

Even thus last night, and two nights more I lay,
And could not win thee, Sleep, by any stealth,
So do not let me wear to-night away.
Without thee what is all the morning's wealth?

William Wordsworth: *To Sleep*

Art thou poor yet hast thou golden slumbers
O sweet content

Thomas Dekker: *The Happy Heart*

SMALL THINGS

I saw a thistledown pass over,
        and in that instant proof without a flaw knew God, whose
    righteousness endures for ever.

Richard Church: *Twentieth Century Psalter*

God is great in the very big things, but greatest in the very little.

St. Augustine

I am done with great things and big things, great institutions and big successes, and I am for those tiny, molecular forces that work for the individual creeping through the crannies of the world like so many soft rootlets or like a capillary oozing of water, yet which, if given time will rend the hardest monument of man's pride.

William James quoted in *Group Psychology*

SOUL

The soul, in popular conception, is already a kind of canary cooped in the cage of real life.

Unattributed

SPIRITUAL

I have sometimes thought that the idea of the "spiritual" in the New Testament might be best explicated by means of the modern concept of "personal". The psychikos and the sarkos are really what belong to the sub-personal realm. The man whose life is confined to these levels is living a sub-personal life. Relationships which never rise above them are not truly personal relationships at all. And no man is living his true life in personal communion with other persons, and above all in that basic personal relationship with God which we call religion.

Donald Baillie: *The Theology of the Sacraments*

STEWARDSHIP (POSSESSION)

'This tent is mine', said Yusef, 'But no more than it is God's; come in and be at peace.'

Lowell

The everlastingness of things - an ironic comment upon your claims to ownership.

Dag Hammarskjold: *Markings*

SUFFERING - GLADLY

At the time of the persecution of Quakers, 1661 "... The prisons were full of them, a continual source of irritation to the magistrates" ... "For this I can say, wrote one, "I never since played the coward but joyfully entered prisons as palaces, telling mine enemies to hold me there as long as they could, and in the prison house I sung praises to my God and esteemed the bolts and locks put upon me as jewels".

Florence Higham: *Faith of our Fathers*

Therefore I bind these lies and slanders to me as an ornament; it belongs to my Christian profession to be vilified, slandered, reproached and reviled; and since all this is nothing else, as my God and my conscience bear witness, I rejoice in reproaches for Christ's sake.

John Bunyan: *Grace Abounding*

When a man of goodwill is afflicted or tempted or troubled with evil thoughts; then he understands better the great need he has of God; without whom he perceives he can do nothing that is good.

Thomas A Kempis: *The Imitation of Christ*
Book 1 Chapter 12

When a man finds that it is his destiny to suffer, he will have to accept his suffering as his task, his single and unique task. He will have to acknowledge the fact that even in suffering he is unique and alone in the universe ... His unique opportunity lies in the way in which he bears his burden

Viktor Frankl quoted in
Prayer Fellowship Handbook 1975

SUGGESTION

Suggestion is too often spoken of as if it were something abnormal; on the contrary, it is one of the most usual things in the world. Very few of the beliefs we hold can be said to rest on really adequate grounds. We believe them because we are told them, or because we imbibed them, without adequate inquiry, from a book. The power of suggestion in the printed page is remarkable. We tend to think that because a thing is printed it must be true.

Stuart Oakden: *American Psychology and Education*

The origin of susceptibility determines some of the characteristics. We accept suggestions from the group as a whole e.g. when we take the tone of an institution from membership of it ... or from someone who impresses us a leader.

Stuart Oakden: *American Psychology and Education*

SURRENDER - SELF

Nothing is enough
No though our all be spent -
Heart's extremest love,
Spirits whole intent,-
Still beyond appeal
Will divine desire
Yet more excellent
Precious cost require,
Of this mortal stuff,-
never be content
Till ourselves be fire.
Nothing is enough.

Laurence Binyon

Strenuously cultivating self-reliance and a self-esteem founded on the just and right, he lived his whole life in happy ignorance of the fact that religion consists in the exact opposite of self-reliance and self-esteem - in total self-surrender to a God who is not merely a very virtuous puritan gentleman, considerably magnified, but a being of a wholly different order.

Aldous Huxley *Grey Eminence* (Of Milton)

Come ill, come well, the Cross, the Crown
The rainbow or the thunder,
I fling my soul and body down
For God to plough them under.

Robert Louis Stevenson: *Youth and Love: I*

It doesn't take much of a man to be a Christian, but it takes all there is of him.

Aldous Huxley quoted by Dean Inge

If a man give all his substance, yet is it nothing...much is wanting: to wit one thing which is most necessary for him. What is that? That having left all he leave himself and go wholly away from himself, and keep no vestige of self love.

Thomas A Kempis: *Imitation of Christ*

When I was thus deliberating upon serving the Lord my God now, as I had long purposed, it was I who willed, I. I, myself. I neither willed entirely, nor willed entirely (sic). Therefore was I at strife with myself, and rent asunder by my self.

St. Augustine: *Confessions*

Self-interest is but the survival of the animal in us. Humanity only begins for man with self surrender.

Henri Frederic Amiel

How far both from muscular heroism and from the soulfully tragic spirit of unselfishness which unctuously adds its little offering to the sponge cake at the Kaffee Klatch is the plain simple fact that a man has given himself completely to something he finds worth living for.

Dag Hammarskjold: *Markings*

SUFFERING - ITS PURPOSE? *see also* PAIN

Pain is the spur to activity and only through pain do we feel ourselves to be fully alive. Without pain we should be lifeless.

Immanuel Kant

"I have known more of God since I came to this bed than through all my life."

Ralph Erskine, living wracked with pain, quoted in
J. S. Stuart's *The Strong Name*

I sympathise a great deal with the listener who replied to every argument on the love of God by the simple question, "What about cancer in fish?"

Evelyn Underhill: *Letters*

How much virtue a man has is best seen on occasions of adversity. For occasions do not make a man fail; but they show what he is.

Thomas A Kempis: *Imitation of Christ*

Those who have suffered a great deal acquire a wide range of vision; their attitude towards others and towards life in general is wise, mature, human.

Svetlana Alliluyeva (Josef Stalin's daughter)

When you come to the bottom you find God.

Neville Talbot

"The darkness," exclaimed Kagawa of Japan, describing what it felt like when he thought he was going blind, "the darkness is a holy of holies of which no-one can rob me. In the darkness I meet God face to face.

J. S. Stuart: *The Strong Name*

The bird of the branch, the lily of the meadow, the stag in the forest, the fish in the sea and countless joyful people sing: God is love. But under all these sopranos as it were a sustained bass part, sounds the De Profundis of the sacrificed God: God is love.

Soren Kierkegarde quoted by J. S. Stuart in *The Strong Name*

In order to understand suffering we have to understand Christ; for it is Christ alone who explains it. Without Christ, suffering remains a horrible and meaningless misfortune. With Christ it becomes an honour and the guarantee of heaven - for those who relieve as well as those who endure.

Group Captain Leonard Cheshire VC DSO DFC

And because he had learnt the lesson that all we prisoners of the
Japanese had to learn if we were to survive - that suffering doesn't
matter ("it doesn't matter" we declare to ourselves, "none of this
matters") because he too has learnt the lesson.

Of Group Captain Leonard Cheshire VC DSO DFC

SYMPATHY

Of Victor Hugo's saintly Bishop Bienvenu, he says: "He understands
how to sit down and hold his peace besides the man who had lost the
wife of his love, the mother who had lost her child. As he knew the
moment for speech, he also knew the moment for silence."

G. T. Jefferies: *This Grace Wherein We Stand*

TEMPTATION

The real Satan is the element in every being which hinders that being
from dying to its selfhood and becoming united with the reality from
which it has been separated.

A. Huxley: *Grey Eminence*

When he angled for Father Joseph's soul, Satan baited his hook with
the noblest temptation; patriotic duty and self-sacrifice. And Joseph
swallowed the hook and gave himself to France with as much ardour as
he had given himself to God. But a man cannot serve two masters.

Aldous Huxley: *Grey Eminence*

Compel your enemy to fight you on your own parade ground.

Lord Fisher quoted by Jowett

For the causes I conceived they were principally two, of which two
also I was deeply convinced all the time this trouble lay upon me. The
first was for that I did not, when I was delivered from the temptation
that went before, still pray to God to keep from the temptations that
were to come; for though, as I can say in truth, my soul was much in
prayer before this trial seized me, yet then I prayed only, or at the most

principally, for the removal of present troubles, and for fresh discoveries of his love in Christ, which I saw afterwards was not enough to do. I also should have prayed that the great God would keep me from evil that was to come.

John Bunyan: *Grace Abounding*

THINKING

We can all do good deeds but very few of us can think good thoughts.

Cesare Pavese: quoted in W. H. Auden's foreword to Dag Hammerskjold's *Markings*

Time But at my back I always hear
Times Winged Chariot hurrying near.

Andrew Marvell: *To his coy mistress*

When as a child I laughed and wept, time crept.
When as a youth I dreamed and talked, time walked
When I became a full grown man, time ran
And later as I older grew, time flew.
Soon I shall find while travelling on, time gone.
Will Christ have saved my soul by then?

From an old clock in Chester Cathedral

TOLERANCE

John and Mary Newton differed in their opinions about Baptists. Mary had written to John critically about them. John's reply came ... "We must try and bear with each other upon this point, till the Lord give us to be of one mind about it, and when he does, I think the change will be in you.

Bernard Martin: *John Newton*

Theodore Buza, Calvin's successor at Geneva stigmatised religious liberty as "a most diabolical dogma, because it means that every man should be left to go to hell in his own way". The same logic was being used by his contemporary, William Allen in England, a papal spokesman who contended strongly that it was against the laws of God and nature to persecute Romists, but that heretics might lawfully be 'coerced'

John Whale: *The Protestant Tradition*

Well-known story of the Presbyterian elder arguing with a Jesuit. "We must agree to differ. We are both trying to serve God: you in your way and I in His.

Geoffrey Parinder: *Comparative Religion*

More charity is shown by the Jewish mystic, Martin Buber, who writes, "All God's names are hallowed".

Geoffrey Parinder: *Comparative Religion*

Rheinhold Niebuhr argued that Christians must learn to live with the tension of having and not having the truth. 'Tolerance' in its truest sense, he maintained, comes when we can have vital convictions which lead to committed actions and at the same time recognise that our own truth is always incomplete and subject to distortion. Living with convictions, we also then live with within the reality of divine forgiveness and with respect for the convictions of those who sincerely differ from us.

James B. Nelson: *Embodiment*

TRUTH

Truth is our only armour in all passages of life and death.

Ralph Waldo Emerson

A Truth that's told with bad intent
    Beats all the lies you can invent.

William Blake: *Auguries of Innocence*

Sympathy, folk often say, is the balm to the troubled spirit; the genuine cure for such troubles is not balm, but the sting of truth.

From a women's paper

Our Lord called himself Truth; he did not call himself tradition.
A famous saying of **Tertullian**

The enquiry of truth, which is the love-making or wooing of it, and
the belief in truth, which is the enjoying of it - is the sovereign good of
human nature
Bacon quoted by S Neill about B. H. Streeter in
The Interpretation of the New Testament

The truth for us is not a terminus: it is the way we have to follow.
Laberthoutére quoted by A. R. Vidler in *Christian Belief*

The mark of real depth is simplicity. If you should say, "This is too profound for me; I cannot grasp it," you are self-deceptive. For you ought
to know that nothing of real importance is too profound for anyone. It
is not because it is too profound, but rather because it is too uncomfort-
able, that you shy away from the truth.
Paul Tillich: *Shaking of the Foundations*

The truth is never pure and rarely simple.
Oscar Wilde: *The Importance of Being Earnest* (Lady Bracknell)

Truth is polygonal. I never feel sure that I have got it until I have
contradicted myself five or six times.
John Ruskin

Truth is tough; it is like a football; you may kick it about all day, but it
remains round and full in the evening.
Oliver Wendell Holmes

To suppose that religious truth can be communicated directly as though
it were mathematical truth or logical method is a shallow blasphemy.
All that religious truth can do is present itself as challenge since the
only way it can be apprehended is by faith.
Unattributed

I had to make do with my own truth, not accept from other what I could not attain on my own.

Carl Jung

The truth that is troubled is the truth which, while itself is terribly certain of being the truth, is essentially concerned with communicating it to others, concerned that they should accept it for their own good, in spite of the fact that the truth does not force itself on them.

Soren Kierkegaard: *Journal* 1849

Kierkegaard's famous definition of truth reads, "An objective uncertainty held fast on the most passionate personal experience is the truth, the highest truth attained for an existing individual". This, he continues is the definition of faith. Tillich later continues, The validating of the truth which appears in a passionate personal experience is based on the relation of the Eternal to the existing individual.

Paul Tillich: *Theology of Culture*

The communication of Christianity must ultimately end in bearing witness, the maseutic method (indirect) can never be final. For truth from the Christian point of view does not lie in the subject, as Socrates understood it, but in the revelation which must be proclaimed.

Soren Kierkegaard: *Journal*

TRADITION

The Archbishop of York, Dr. Ramsey told The York diocesan conference recently that in an Indian community in Labrador people were still praying for Queen Victoria. When they were urged to come up to date and pray for the reigning sovereign they protested that they had from the first prayed for Queen Victoria and wished to continue.

S. S. *Chronicle* 3rd December 1959

TREASURE IN HEAVEN

'Twas glorious to me to see his exaltation, and the worth and prevalency of all his benefits, and that because I could now look from myself to him and would reckon that all those graces of God that were now green on me were yet like those cracked groats and fourpence half-pennies that rich men carry in their purses when their gold is in their trunks at home. Oh I saw my gold was in my trunk at home - in Christ My Lord and Saviour! Now Christ was all - my righteousness, all my sanctification and all my redemption.

John Bunyan: *Grace Abounding*

UNITY

We would be one in hatred of all wrong
One in our love of all things sweet and fair
One with the joy that breaketh into song
One with the grief that trembleth into prayer
One in the power that makes the children free
To follow truth, and thus to follow thee.

J. C. Chadwick: *Congregational Praise* No. 554

In necessary things, unity; in doubtful things, liberty; in all things, charity.

Richard Baxter

UNSELFISHNESS

Weeds are the blight of the fields, the blight of this generation is self-seeking.

Buddhist saying

It is a matter of experience and observation that actions undertaken by ordinary unregenerate people, sunk in their selfhood and without spiritual insight, seldom do much good.

Aldous Huxley: *Grey Eminence*

UNTRUTHFULNESS

Talking of an acquaintance of ours, whose narratives, which abounded in envious and interesting topicks, were unhappily found to be very fabulous; I mentioned Lord Mansfield's having said to me, "Suppose we believe one half of what he tells". Johnson, "Aye, but we don't know which half to believe. By his lying we lose not only reverence for him, but all comfort in his conversation".

James Boswell: *Life of Samuel* Johnson 1783

VALUE

What is a cynic? A man who knows the price of everything and the value of nothing.

Oscar Wilde: *Lady Windermere's Fan*

It is a salutary reflection that the reason why the priest and the Levite did not stop to help the wounded man on the Jericho road was not that they were hard-hearted hypocrites but that they had an urgent appointment to attend the Committee for the Relief of Distressed Travellers.

David H. C. Read: *The Communication of the Gospel*

The cost of a thing is the amount of life it requires to be exchanged for it, immediately or in the long run.

Henry David Thoreau

Where feelings are concerned, the same thing happens to me as happened to the Englishman who got into financial difficulties when no one could change his five pound note.

Soren Kierkegaard: *Journal* 1844

VISION

Alexander Fleming (the discoverer of Penicillin) once said the greatest need for scientists was vision. "Unless they have vision they can do comparatively little with their formulae." And in his first days in Dr. Wright's laboratory at St. Mary's he began to show that he the right kind of vision for a research scientist.

John Rowland: *The Penicillin Man*

WILL

No, Lord, I ask no conscious enjoyment of Thy gifts save that I may be able to say in all honesty, though without sweetness of feeling, that I would die sooner than give up faith, hope and love. The highest point of religion is to be content with bare, dry acts, performed solely by the superior will.

St. Frances of Sales

WILLPOWER

Do what lieth in thy power; and God will help thy good will.

Thomas A Kempis: *Imitation of Christ*

Will is a desire that has become dominant. A wish is an ineffectual desire.

Paul Bull: *Lectures on Preaching*

WILL OF GOD

In old Chinese art there is just one outstanding object, perhaps a flower or a scroll.; Everything else is subordinate to this one beautiful thing. An integrated life is like that. What is that one flower? It is the will of God. But to know his will and to do it calls for absolute sincerity, absolute honesty with oneself, and it means using one's mind to the best of one's ability ... with me religion is a very simple thing. It means to try with all my heart and soul and strength to do the will of God.

Mme Chiang Kai Shek: *S. S. Chronicle July 1943*

I particularly like what you said about physical suffering; that it is God's will and yet also is never his will. That paradox has to be held onto all the time - so that we can accept even evil and imperfection as penetrated, in spite of themselves by God's over-ruling will and grace and turned thus to His final purpose though still remaining, in themselves and until redeemed, contrary to his intrinsic will for life.

Evelyn Underhill: *Letter to Maisie Spens*

Why that war? Why my subsequently lawless life? To understand it, to understand the whole of the Master's will, is not in my power. But to do his will that is written in my conscience, that is in my power; that I know for certain, and when I am fulfilling it I have sureness and peace.

Leo Tolstoy: *Resurrection*

The will of God is not a system of rules that is established from the outset; it is something new and different in each different situation in life, and for this reason a man must ever examine anew what the will of God is.

Dietrich Bonhoeffer; quoted John V. Taylor's
The Go-between God

The religious person is accustomed to the thought of not being sole master in his own house. He believes that God, and not he himself, decides in the end. But how many of us would dare to let the will of God decide, and which of us would not feel embarrassed if he had to say how far the decision came from God himself.

Carl Jung: *The Undiscovered Self*

The doing of God's will is what gives meaning to every situation whether it is happy or revolting. Suffering is given a Christian meaning by being accepted as the sphere in which it is appointed that I serve God at this time.

J. N. Ward: *The Use of Prayer*

WISDOM

Knowledge is proud that he has learned so much,
Wisdom is humble that he knows no more.

Unattributed

Witnessing And indeed I did often say before the Lord, that if I be hanged up presently before their eyes, it would be a means to waken them, and confirm them in the truth, and I gladly should be contented.

John Bunyan: *Grace Abounding*

In all such conversations (i. e. converting by controversial method) Susil
Rudra and the leading Indian Christians in Delhi expressed the strong
opinion that silent influence, carrying with it the fragrance of a true
Christian life, was worth all the propagandist teaching in the world.
It was of very great interest to me to find in later years, that Mahatma
Ghandi has stated, in almost identical terms, the same view as Susil.
The bloom of the rose, he said, does not need to proclaim itself loudly
to the world. Its very presence is the witness of its own sweetness. So,
he added, a Christian life, that grows silently like the rose, shedding its
perfume silently on every side, is the truest witness to Christ.

WAR

War is a detestable thing. If you had seen one day of war you would
pray God you might never see another.

Duke of Wellington

WONDER

There are many men and women who would appear to have lost the
capacity for wonder: what does it all mean? Why am I here, and what
am I? Like men who have grown accustomed to the beauty and mystery
of a sunset and looking at it merely think, "the refraction of light by the
earth's atmosphere", so they accept life as a stale phenomenon, a story
that has been told so often that it ceases to have any meaning.

Kenneth Walker: *Diagnosis of Man*

It is a positive start for philosophy when Aristotle says that philosophy
begins with wonder, not as in our day, with doubt.

Unattributed

THE WORLD

The world is a bridge, so pass over it and do not inhabit it..
>Ascetic teachings attributed to Jesus as taken
>from Islamic literature.

The world's no blot for us,
Nor blank, it means intensely and means good:
To find its meaning is my meat and drink.
>**Robert Browning:** *Fra Lippo Lippi*

WORSHIP

And whenever you leave the silence of
that happy meeting place
You must mind and bear the image of
Your Master in your face
>**Ellen Lakshmi Goren:** *In the Secret of His Presence*
>quoted by C. F. Andrews in *Christ in the Silence*

To believe in God is to go down on your knees.
>**Martin Luther** quoted by J. S. Whale in *The Protestant*

Worship is offer and response.
>**Evelyn Underhill:** *Worship* quoted by D. S. Hubery in
>*Teaching the Christian Faith Today*

When you reflect after communion, "What have I done today?" said
Forsyth, "say to yourself: I have done more than on any busiest day of
the week. I yielded myself to take part with the Church in Christ's
finished work of redemption, which is more than the making of the
world."
>**P.T. Forsyth:** quoted in symposium
>*About Worship* by Martin Shepherd

The world is imprisoned by its own activity except when its actions are performed as worship of God. Therefore you must perform every action sacramentally and be free from all attachment to results.

Bhagavad Gita quoted by F. C. Happold, *Mysticism*

To worship is to quicken the conscience by the holiness of God, to feed the mind by the truth of God, to purge the imagination by the beauty of God, to open the heart to the love of God, to devote the will to the purpose of God. All this is gathered up in that emotion which which most cleanses us from selfishness because it is the most selfless of all emotions - adoration.

William Temple: *Daily Readings*

Sunday 18th June 1939 Service in Riverside Church. Quite unbearable. Text: a saying from James(!) about "accepting an horizon", how one gets an horizon, namely God as man's necessary Horizon.

The whole thing was a respectable, self-indulgent, self-satisfied, religious celebration. This sort of idolatrous religion stirs up the flesh, which is accustomed to being kept in check by the Word of God. Such sermons make for libertinism, egotism, indifference. Do people not know that they can get on as well, if not better, without "religion" if only there were not God himself and His Word.

Dietrich Bonhoeffer: *The Way to Freedom*

Printed in Great Britain
by Amazon